Praise

"John DiJulius is leading a radical rethinking of customer service that can revolutionize your business. This book will become the new standard for how we think about customer service and competitive advantage."
—*Joe Calloway, author of* **Be the Best at What Matters Most**

"John DiJulius always has something insightfully practical to help businesses up their service game. His latest book is no exception, offering exceptional advice."
—*James H. Gilmore, author of* **The Experience Economy**

"DiJulius's commitment to 'changing the world' comes at a time in business history when it is desperately needed. Advancements in technology and efficiency, coupled with an expanding global economy, have led to an unparalleled competitive landscape. Ultimately, service is the only differentiator. *The Customer Service Revolution* is a straightforward blueprint for building sustainable advantage in any industry and is a must-read for anyone looking to build world-class experiences."
—*Derek Kaivani, director of PwC Experience, PricewaterhouseCoopers*

"John DiJulius is the real deal. He will show you how to create a customer service revolution so powerful that your price will become irrelevant. He is a master at creating the exclusive experience and is the world's expert on dazzling customers. Do yourself a favor and drop everything you're doing and read this book—it's worth it!"
—*Rory Vaden, cofounder of Southwestern Consulting and* **New York Times** *best-selling author of* **Take the Stairs**

"John takes customer service from thought to action—truly a difference maker for all!"
—*David Mortensen, president and cofounder of Anytime Fitness Worldwide*

"John relates an amazing amount of practical real world examples that can be applied in your efforts to launch a customer service revolution in your business as I have in my direct work with John."
—*Michael Coburn, Head of Customer Facing Supply Chain, Nestlé USA*

Previous books by John R. DiJulius III

Secret Service: Hidden Systems That Deliver
Unforgettable Customer Service
(AMACOM, 2003)

What's the Secret? To Providing
a World-Class Customer Experience
(Wiley, 2008)

THE

CUSTOMER SERVICE REVOLUTION

*Overthrow Conventional Business,
Inspire Employees, and Change the World*

JOHN R. DiJULIUS III

GREENLEAF
BOOK GROUP PRESS

Published by Greenleaf Book Group Press
Austin, Texas
www.gbgpress.com

Distributed by Greenleaf Book Group
For ordering information or special discounts for bulk purchases, please contact Greenleaf Book Group at PO Box 91869, Austin, TX 78709, 512.891.6100.

Design and composition by Greenleaf Book Group and Kim Lance
Cover design by Greenleaf Book Group and Kim Lance
Cover images: RTimages/iStock Collection/Thinkstock

Cataloging-in-Publication data
DiJulius, John R., 1964-
   The customer service revolution : overthrow conventional business, inspire employees, and change the world / John R. DiJulius III.—First edition.
      pages : illustrations ; cm
   Issued also as an ebook.
   Includes bibliographical references.
   1. Customer services. 2. Customer relations—Management. 3. Employees—Training of. 4. Corporate culture. I. Title.
HF5415.5 .D55 2015
658.8/12   2014938305

ISBN: 978-1-62634-129-6

Part of the Tree Neutral® program, which offsets the number of trees consumed in the production and printing of this book by taking proactive steps, such as planting trees in direct proportion to the number of trees used: www.treeneutral.com

TreeNeutral®

Printed in the United States of America on acid-free paper
15 16 17 18 19 20   10 9 8 7 6 5 4 3
First Edition
Other Edition(s)
eBook ISBN: 978-1-62634-130-2

To my three amazing sons and best friends:
Johnni, Cal, and Bo

CONTENTS

WHAT IS A CUSTOMER SERVICE REVOLUTION?
Your biggest competitive advantage

When you are inspired by some great purpose, some extraordinary project, all your thoughts break their bonds: Your mind transcends limitations, your consciousness expands in every direction, and you find yourself in a new, great and wonderful world.

—*PATAÑJALI*

The Great Recession

From 2008 to 2010, the United States experienced some of the worst economic times in our lives. The housing bubble burst and the stock market plummeted. We saw the demise of financial institutions. Foreclosures, job loss, and bankruptcy were rampant. What became known as the Great Recession ultimately affected the entire world economy. While much of it was devastating, some good came out of these troubling economic times. Believe it or not, there were many companies that survived significantly better than their competition and businesses in general, and as a result, they emerged better and stronger than before. How? Because in any economy—especially a down economy—Customer loyalty is your strongest asset! It took the recession to shine a spotlight on these thriving companies and what they had in common: a fanatical obsession on the Customer experience.

Customer service became hip, and more and more smart leaders and management teams started focusing on improving the experiences their companies delivered. As a result, over the past several years, overall Customer service satisfaction has improved.[1] A revolution has started, a Customer service revolution, and it has gained incredible momentum. It is not only changing the way businesses operate, but it is also having a profound ripple effect in numerous other areas.

What a Customer service revolution really is

The DiJulius Group (TDG) is a Customer service consulting firm headquartered in Cleveland, Ohio. TDG's purpose is "to change the world by creating a Customer service revolution." We are so proud that hundreds of organizations all over the world have adopted this as a major part of their business strategy, as they distance themselves from the competition. However, for it to be truly successful—so it is not just another mantra, annual theme, platitude, or flavor of the month—it is critical you understand what creating a Customer service revolution really means:

> A radical overthrow of conventional business mentality designed to transform what employees and Customers experience. This shift produces a culture that permeates into people's personal lives, at home, and in the community, which in turn provides the business with higher sales, morale, and brand loyalty—making price irrelevant.[2]

Let's break that definition down to its core:

"A radical overthrow of conventional business mentality . . ." This is an approach or mind-set to business unlike what anyone has ever thought about previously. It's radical and unconventional. This unique concept consumes businesses leaders and entrepreneurs, energizes them, and ultimately inspires them to create breakthrough companies, products, services, and ultimately, experiences.

". . . designed to transform what Customers experience . . ." Revolutionary companies create "experience epiphanies" that fill a gap Customers didn't know existed. World-class Customer service companies create enduring relationships and personal connections.

". . . and employees experience." Experience it forward. What employees experience, Customers will. The best marketing is happy, engaged employees. Your Customers will never be any happier than your employees.

"This shift produces a culture that permeates into people's personal lives, at home, and in the community . . ." Genuine hospitality is not something you do; it is something that is in you. It is something in all areas of your life—with your Customers, employees, family, and neighbors. Service to others is what we owe for the privilege of living on this earth. It is the very purpose of life and not something you do only when it is convenient.

". . . which in turns provides the business with higher sales, morale, and brand loyalty . . ." The only businesses surviving with long-term sustainability are the ones fanatical about differentiating themselves through the Customer experience they deliver.

". . . making price irrelevant." Based on the experience your Customers consistently receive, they have no idea what your competition charges.

Making price irrelevant

I love this phrase, especially because it sparks conversation and debate. Is it possible to actually make price irrelevant? Absolutely! What it does not mean is that you can double your prices or even raise them 20 percent tomorrow and not lose a Customer. What it does mean is that, based on the experience your business consistently provides to your Customers, a significantly fewer number of Customers will be price-shopping you. Every one of us is price sensitive to some degree. Typically, with the majority of companies where we do business, we know how much they charge versus how much we can get the same thing from somewhere else. However, all of us have a few businesses we are loyal to because of something that they repeatedly do for us or give us, or because of how they make us feel; thus, we have no idea what their competitors charge, nor do we care. Where do you compete, in the price wars, or experience wars? I prefer to compete in the experience wars—a lot less competition. Many times when a Customer complains about the price, it isn't because they were not willing to pay for it; it is because the experience didn't warrant it. Price is something you offer when you have nothing else. In fact, 85 percent of US consumers say they would pay 5 to 25 percent more to ensure a superior experience.[3] Think about the companies that literally revolutionized their industries, companies like Zappos, Amazon, Starbucks, Chick-fil-A, Southwest Airlines, and Apple. Each line of that Customer service revolution definition applies to their radical approach to trashing the traditional industry mold and rewriting history.

I invite you to join the revolution! Turn the page!

STATE OF SERVICE

The new rules to dominating your industry

A revolution is the ability to rally a group of people around a cause, so committed to seeing it through because it will benefit and change the world.

Are you part of the Customer service crisis, or the Customer service revolution?

Strong economic times can disguise a company's weaknesses, and too often businesses with poor fundamentals can survive and sometimes grow for the short term. However, eventually the rubber meets the road, and only the businesses built on the premise that employee and Customer loyalty are their strongest assets are the ones that thrive and emerge as market leaders for the long term. These businesses realize that Customer service training is an investment, not an expense.

Not only have the rules changed, but the entire game is different

Here are the three biggest influences on Customer service, which are continuing to evolve the way companies do business today:

1. Social media

2. It is all about time

3. Customer Xperience leader

The biggest influence on Customer service in fifty years

Technology has always changed the way business operates. The Internet opened up an incredible dynamic and an opportunity for information, marketing, and sharing. The biggest influence, no question, is social media, on so many different levels. Social media has turned Customer service upside down. Today, more than ever before, Customers are informed and empowered, and expect personalization and quicker responses. Remember the days when the business controlled the communication, actually controlled the customer? The business would decide if you would get to talk to someone, who that someone would be, on their own timetable. Not any more, the Customer is in complete control of communication, since now your Customer has instant access to social media, which means instant access to thousands of people. Companies need to make sure they have proper procedures in place to react when a Customer reaches out on social media. If not, then you run the risk of a potential nightmare. Social media is not just for marketing and promotions. I am actually turned off by companies that only shamelessly promote themselves. Social media is also a way to communicate with your Customers, answer their questions, and respond quickly to their complaints. Every business has to have someone managing what is being said about its brand in the social media channels. Share insights, educate your Customers, show them resources, and find ways to help others—ways that don't just benefit you.

> *You earn business by being generous*
> *with your knowledge and resources without*
> *asking for anything in return.*

Every business is under a microscope now

Companies can no longer hide if they deliver unacceptable Customer experiences and treat people disrespectfully. They will be out of business; it's that simple. I ask my employees, "How would you behave if CNN were on site shooting a documentary?" With smartphones, everyone now has a video camera in hand.

What used to be "word of mouth" is now "word of mouse"

According to a recent report from Fleishman-Hillard, the company found that 89 percent of consumers turn to Google, Bing, or another search engine to find information on products, services, or businesses prior to making purchases.[4] What you do well and not so well will be broadcast to hundreds, if not thousands, of potential Customers. They expect your company to be easy to contact and quick to respond.

> *You are creating either brand ambassadors,*
> *or brand terrorists doing brand assassination.*

People do not expect you to be perfect, but how you handle imperfection better be. We need to be zero risk to deal with. Zero risk does not mean you will never screw up, but it does mean you will admit when you drop the ball. As a result, Customers can become more loyal because of the way you handled the problem.

The Customer rebellion

All this has resulted in the Customer service crisis. Companies spend millions creating and advertising their brands, yet the Customer's experience is what drives Customer perception.

Consumers have less patience and are more outspoken than ever before. Customers are no longer tolerating subpar service, indifference, and unempathetic businesses, and they are standing up for themselves. They won't take it anymore, which has resulted in the Customer rebellion. For hundreds of years, the best form of advertising was word of mouth. Today, it is word of mouse. Social media represents a gigantic power shift back to the consumer. Now consumers can share their displeasure with thousands of others just with a click of a button. It takes twenty years to build a reputation and five minutes to ruin it. Also, the Internet and technology have made Customers more demanding, and they expect information, answers, products, responses, and resolutions sooner than ASAP. As Sam Walton, founder of Walmart said, "There's only one boss, the customer, and he can fire everybody in the company from the chairman on down, simply by spending money somewhere else or on something else."

Power to the people

A decade ago we saw a massive decline in face-to-face interaction due to the dramatic increase in e-commerce. However, today, social media has brought back a huge shift of people-to-people interaction. Consumers have more direct, daily contact with other consumers than has ever been possible. More contact means more sharing of information, gossiping, exchanging, engaging—in short, more word of mouth. An article titled "How Social Media Are Amplifying Customer Outrage" that was on CNN.com illustrates the power of the Customer's voice today. In 2011, Netflix had a severe fallout. The Internet magnified the situation. Overnight, the company decided to increase its prices 60 percent. As a result, Netflix had to staff hundreds of extra Customer service reps to handle the incoming calls of irate Customers. It didn't stop there. It also had to deal with four thousand negative posts on its blog. If that wasn't enough, the company got eighty thousand posts on its Facebook page! These social media outlets allow Customers to voice their dissatisfaction and gain momentum like never before.[5]

Satisfying the Customer pays big

There is only one true growth: growth that occurs because Customers love doing business with you and become brand evangelists for you. Brand evangelists don't just come back. They don't simply recommend you—they insist that their friends do business with you. The American Customer Satisfaction Index (ACSI) reached a record high in the third quarter of 2013. Stock price and ACSI scores tend to move together for individual companies.[6]

According to research from the University of Michigan, Customer satisfaction is directly linked to stock market performance. Companies with high scores on the ACSI produce higher stock returns than competitors and greatly outperform the stock market.

The study examined the correlation between Customer satisfaction and financial success. Over a twelve-year period (2000–2012), the stock value of the companies that had the highest Customer satisfaction scores went up 390 percent, whereas the average stock in the S&P 500 went down 7 percent! So, if in 2000 you invested $100,000 in top Customer satisfaction companies, your cumulative return would have been $390,000. Compare that with investing that same $100,000 in the S&P 500: you would have ended up with only $93,000, a loss of $7,000.[7]

E-commerce tops brick and mortar

The good news is, Customer satisfaction with retailers is at an all-time high. The bad news is, online retailers consistently outperform brick-and-mortar businesses in Customer satisfaction. Retailers wonder and complain why Customers are "show-rooming" (window-shopping at stores and then making the purchase online) and defecting to the Internet for their purchases. Now they know why. In fact, of the nine retail companies with the worst ACSI scores, only one was an online retailer, Netflix.[8]

It's about *time*

Speed of time and speed of service are as critical to the Customer experience as anything. Everyone in the organization has to understand how valuable time is to the Customer. It is vital that businesses demonstrate to their Customers that their time is always regarded as a critical resource.

It doesn't matter what industry you are in today, companies like Google, Zappos, and Amazon have affected your business. They have affected the expectations of your Customers. It is all about time, and the world of the Internet has made everything instantaneous, from information and answers to questions to products in people's hands. Today a friend can recommend a good book for you to read and within thirty seconds it is in your hands on your

Kindle. There are companies like Zappos and other great retailers that can have a product at your door the next morning if you order it by 6 p.m. This has not only changed Customers' expectations for everyone they do business with, but it has also changed their level of patience. Customers expect phone calls and emails returned the same day, as well as support and resolutions to their issues. They expect you to find them the product they are looking for, not to be told they can go home and search the Internet. In his book *The Amazement Revolution*, author Shep Hyken shares a story on how the Four Seasons Hotel understands the critical importance of its Customers' time:

> It's time. The wealthy Customers consistently report to researchers that they are working harder and longer hours than ever before, that they experience serious stress in their lives because of the lack of available time to do everything they want to do, and that they flat-out resent being kept waiting . . .
>
> The guest's time will always be respected . . . You are the most important priority for me right now, and I am not putting any other task in front of the task of serving you.[9]

Wanted: Chief customer officer

The fastest growing C-level position popping up in the corporate world is chief customer officer (CCO), also known as the chief Xperience officer (CXO). With the old paradigm, the Customer service duties were left on the plate of the director of training, human resources (HR), or the chief marketing officer.[10] Regardless of your company's size, someone in your organization has to be in charge of the Customer experience and all that goes with it. I am not talking about the head of the Customer service department—that is, call centers. I am talking about someone who oversees the entire company's Customer service, every department. That someone should not be the president, CEO, or owner, but someone who reports directly to them. Companies have heads of operations, marketing, accounting, sales, and human resources, but our second biggest asset (other than our employees) is our Customer. How happy they are is determined by the Customer experience we deliver. Until recently, the vast majority of companies had no one in charge of the Customer or their experience. Regardless of your company's size, you need to have someone who loses sleep at night over the Customer and how every department and all employee training affects the Customer's experience.

Customer eXperience Executive Academy

With the rapid growth of the CCO and CXO positions in businesses today, a tough challenge has been getting these executives the proper Customer service training needed to lead an entire company's experience and all the components that go along with that responsibility. As a result of this demand, educational resources like the Customer eXperience Executive Academy (CXEA.org), have been created so companies from all over the world can send their Customer service leaders for comprehensive training and certification on all the facets and responsibilities that fall under Customer experience.

3

SERVICE APTITUDE
The game changer

It is not the employees' responsibility to have high Service Aptitude; it is the company's job to teach it to them.

Who's to blame?

If your employee disappoints your Customer, whose fault is that? Typically, the blame is placed on the employee for using poor judgment or being indifferent to the Customer. However, 99 percent of the time blame should be placed on the company or supervisor for putting someone in a position they were not qualified to handle. Most companies have their new employees go through technical training only, and when they end up delivering poor Customer service, management gets frustrated with that employee's decision making. It is not their fault!

Most would agree that the hospitality side (how our Customers are treated and cared for) is just as important as the technical/operational side of what the Customer receives. However, our training contradicts that. We would never think of having an accountant, lawyer, nurse, doctor, hairdresser, or technician perform work without the proper technical training, certification, and licensing. Yet most companies have little to zero Customer service certification. To my knowledge, there is no college major in Customer experience that prepares our next generation of workforce on how to have strong Customer service skills.

Service Aptitude

Companies don't engage emotionally with their Customers—their employees do. If you want to create a memorable company, you have to fill your company with memorable people. The quality of your Customer service, and the level of your organization's Customer service, comes down to one thing and one thing only: The Service Aptitude of every employee you have. From the CEO to the account executive, sales clerk, call center, receptionist, corporate office support team, to every front-line employee—it's all about Service Aptitude!!! The most critical component in building a world-class Customer experience culture is the Service Aptitude of every individual employee in your company.

> Service Aptitude: A person's ability to recognize opportunities to exceed Customers' expectations, regardless of the circumstances.[11]

Service Aptitude scarcity

No one is born with it; it is not innate. The vast majority of the workforce has extremely low Service Aptitude, especially when they are entering the workforce after finishing school, regardless if that is high school, college, graduate school, or a trade school. As a result of poor training and paranoid management, many employees, including management, don't have high Service Aptitude even after years of working. And sadly, a high percentage of senior-level executives continue to have low Service Aptitude during their careers. Why? Why is high Service Aptitude so rare? What dictates it, and what impacts it? There are three things that shape everyone's Service Aptitude:

1. Life experiences
2. Past work experiences
3. Current work experiences

Life experiences are a significant factor in people's Service Aptitude level, especially in the younger workforce. Think about home environment, groups of friends, and life experiences growing up. Frontline employees' standard of living typically does not afford them the opportunity to fly first class, stay at five-star resorts, drive a luxury automobile, and enjoy other higher-end experiences. Yet we, as managers, expect those same employees to be able to deliver world-class service to clients, guests, patients, or whomever we call our Customers, who may be accustomed to these types of experiences. It doesn't make any sense.

Previous work experiences have a major impact on a person's Service Aptitude. Think about how small the percentage is of organizations that are truly world-class at Customer service. It is a good bet that most of your frontline employees have previously worked for an average or less-than-average Customer service company, which means that not only were they not trained on what excellent service looks like, but they were brainwashed by a policy-driven, ironfisted manager who taught them that Customers are out to take advantage of businesses.

Current work experiences dictate the current state of an employee's Service Aptitude. Nearly every company states on paper, plaques, and its website how it has a Customer-first philosophy, but how many really back that up? New employees typically get initial training on a company's operational processes—product knowledge, how to do the fundamentals of the job, and so on—but very little if any Customer service or soft-skill training is invested up front. Actions speak louder than words.

The Golden Rule is a dangerous Customer service compass

I love the Golden Rule: *treat others the way you would like to be treated*. However, you don't want your frontline employees treating Customers the way they want to be treated. Let's consider my oldest son, Johnni. He is a junior at Ohio State University. Johnni is the nicest young man you could ever meet. However, if you hired him today and threw him in a Customer-facing, frontline position and told him to treat Customers the way he likes to be treated, you would probably see him greet people with, "Hey, what's up, dude?" He just may give them a fist bump, and you might have to ask him to pull up his sagging pants higher than he is wearing them. He is a typical college student; this is what they do. It's how they like to be treated. Now give him a few weeks of soft-skill training and he will be one of the most genuine, hospitable employees you have. For servicing Customers, it is the platinum rule that we need to focus on: treating others how *they* enjoy being treated.

It isn't their fault; they don't know any better

I have this sweet niece whom I bugged for years to come work for me. She has those qualities any business would love in an employee who comes in contact with Customers: always smiling, very friendly, and outgoing. We were celebrating a holiday at my house and I asked her what she was doing. She said she had been working at a restaurant as a hostess/receptionist. She also explained that one of her responsibilities was to police the restrooms. I told her that the cleanliness of the restrooms was so important to the image of the restaurant. She said, "No, that's not what I mean by policing the bathrooms. My boss says it is my job not to let anyone use the restrooms unless they are paying Customers." My eyes lit up. I said, "Really?" She replied, "Yes, we even have a sign on the door that says so. In fact, last week I saw someone who hadn't purchased anything headed to the restroom, so I ran after him and made him leave." I was horrified! This is my sweet adorable niece with the same DNA as I, and with the same last name. How could she think like this?

You may be thinking how wrong I am about my niece being a wonderful employee. Actually, she may be too good of an employee. Her boss (sadly, the owner of the restaurant) has told her, "Your job is to not let people take advantage of us," and she says, "Okay!" And she does what she is told, protects the business like she has been instructed. Each of us has plenty of employees currently working for us who have worked elsewhere and have been influenced by other bosses who don't think like world-class Customer service companies and leaders do. They are more concerned that people are out to take advantage of them than they are of taking care of the Customer. It is not a new employee's responsibility to have high Service Aptitude; it is the company's job to teach it to them.

Executive sponsorship

It is a proven fact that any big initiative, project, or revolution has to have the support of the senior leadership team; otherwise it will be considered "flavor of the month" or "management by bestseller."

Customer service has to be as important as finance, sales,

operations, and technology. It needs to be talked about at board meetings and strategic planning sessions, with leaders and everyone else in the company, including frontline employees. The senior leadership team has to provide the necessary resources to create long-lasting change. That isn't just increasing the budget for Customer service. It is having someone in charge of the project—that is, a Chief Xperience Officer (CXO)—who is dedicated and loses sleep at night over the Customer experience program and the results (see chapter 2). People must be able to tell that the leadership of the company is truly committed and passionate about the Customer experience. I always like to say, if my employees can finish my sentences when I address them, then I am doing a good job with my vision and message.

Service Aptitude starts at the top

Typically, when I get done speaking at a conference, I get one of two types of questions from attendees.

First, "Can we really get our frontline employees to buy into this and treat Customers better?" I respond, "Absolutely. If you follow the plan, you will create a world-class Customer experience organization. It takes time, but be relentless and follow the plan." The other question I get is, "How can I get my boss/president/CEO to buy into this?" And I respond, "Have him or her come to my next presentation, or get them the book." But what I am really thinking is, *You are sunk.* If the top people can't passionately believe in the Customer experience, the company will never embody it. What do Howard Schultz (Starbucks), Walt Disney (Walt Disney World), Tony Hsieh (Zappos), Richard Branson (Virgin Airlines), Steve Jobs (Apple), Horst Schulze (the Ritz-Carlton), Truett Cathy (Chick-fil-A), Herb Kelleher (Southwest Airlines), John Nordstrom (Nordstrom), and Jeff Bezos (Amazon), have in common? Each of these leaders obsessed over their company's Customer experience, down to the smallest detail. They passionately articulated their vision for world-class experience every time they spoke, to anyone and everyone who would listen. And their companies are all known for world-class Customer service. Service Aptitude starts at the very top.

The Customer service hall of shame

Just the same, for every poor Customer service company, you can typically track the reason it is so bad back to the lack of Service Aptitude of its leader. The CEO of Spirit Airlines is a perfect example. Spirit Airlines is the most-complained-about airline in the United States. To which Spirit CEO Ben Baldanza said, "That's irrelevant!" Being the worst at Customer service in the airline industry isn't easy. Very few people like airline companies (except if you are a Southwest and Virgin Airlines passenger). You have to be pretty bad to be the worst. Spirit reached a new low back in 2012 when a seventy-six-year-old Vietnam veteran and former marine tried to get his $197 back for a flight he purchased before he found out he had terminal esophageal cancer. After being told by his doctor not to fly from Florida to Atlantic City, airline officials told him to forget it, and Baldanza reaffirmed the company's hard line in an exclusive FoxNews.com interview. "A lot of our Customers buy that insurance and what Mr. Meekins asked us to do was essentially give him the benefit of the insurance when he didn't purchase the insurance," Baldanza said. "Had we done that, I think it really would've been cheating all the people who actually bought the insurance . . . and I think that's fundamentally unfair." We are talking about $197! Social media exploded over this controversial topic. Within days, there was a "Boycott Spirit Airlines" page that earned over thirty-six thousand likes. Spirit Airlines also charges its

Customers extra for each additional service or amenity, including a $100 fee for carry-on bags stored in overhead bins.[12]

When a significant portion of a company's profits come from hidden or penalty fees, that company only survives by getting very good at handing out such punishments. That is exactly what damaged the reputation of the banking and cell phone industries in the late 1990s and early 2000s. This is something called the "gotcha economy," which rewards being sneaky and cheating the Customer.

Stupidity fee

Michael O'Leary, head of Ryanair (headquartered in Dublin, Ireland), called his Customers "idiots." O'Leary was speaking specifically about fliers who fail to print their boarding passes before they arrive at the airport, and are therefore forced to pay a €60 fee. The issue came to a head after a mom had to pay a €360 penalty fee to print boarding passes so her family could fly home from Spain to Britain. She aired her concerns on Facebook and got hundreds of thousands of likes. O'Leary responded to the posts:

> We think Mrs. McLeod should pay 60 euros for being so stupid. She wasn't able to print her boarding card because, as you know, there are no Internet cafes in Alicante, no hotels where they could print them out for you, and you couldn't get to a fax machine so some friend at home can print them and fax them to you.[13]

Policy versus personalize

As a Customer, I don't want to hear "No, it is not our policy." If you actually think about it, policy is the complete opposite of personalize. I don't care about your policy; your policy is a blanket statement that was written for the masses.

Guidelines, not policy

A John Robert's Spa Customer contacted me because she was upset we wouldn't allow her to return makeup of ours that she'd had an allergic reaction to. I asked the manager, someone very good at Customer service, why she didn't give the Customer a refund. My manager responded with, "Because our policy is . . ." I explained that in certain cases, we must make exceptions, like this one, because the Customer was allergic to the product. My manager replied, "But if we return it for her, then everyone will start returning makeup." I laughed. Just because we return one person's makeup, that doesn't mean that we are going to get a rush of Customers bringing in their makeup for full refunds. I have found that this type of nervous, protective mentality is not unusual, and not only at the front line—management can often think like this as well. I always tell my employees I would rather them be naïve than paranoid.

At first, when my team members made poor decisions like this, resulting in upsetting our Customers, I would always get frustrated and think, *Why do I have people that do these types of things?* That is when it hit me: this manager was doing what she was taught to do—follow company policies. It wasn't her fault that she was disappointing the Customer. It was the company's fault—my fault! Most employees only see things as black and white and often do not feel they can deviate from company rules. That is when I decided to drop the word "policy" and replace it with "guidelines."

Policy can kill your brand

Management needs to have high Service Aptitude. The DiJulius Group works with a company that has a chain of auto-repair facilities throughout the United States. The following story happened at one of their locations, before we started working with them. A Customer came in to get his vehicle repaired, with a bill that totaled more than $800. While the Customer waited for his vehicle to be repaired, he purchased a cup of coffee at a café that was part of this vehicle-repair shop. However, the Customer felt his coffee was too cold and told the manager that he wanted his money back (only a few dollars). The manager said no because the "policy" is they don't return half-consumed beverages. The Customer demanded his money back for his coffee, so the manager proceeded to call the police. This is for a cup of coffee that costs the business a few cents, and the Customer had already spent over $800.

Poor Service Aptitude can destroy a great Customer service system every day

A national restaurant chain, one which is consistently ranked at the top in Customer satisfaction in their food category, created an excellent Secret Service system, a way to capture Customer intelligence to personalize the experience (more on Secret Service in chapter 8). When its Customers placed their orders and paid for them, the restaurant started having its employees ask for the Customer's first name or had them capture something about the Customer (e.g., blue shirt). This Customer intelligence was then entered into the point-of-sale software and would print out on the receipt that was taped to the Customer's order, so the employee could use this information and personalize it by saying things like "Jack, your meatball sub is ready"—a far cry from the traditional experience of hearing someone shout out "Meatball sub!"

While that is a great system, an employee with extremely low Service Aptitude and horrible judgment decided to type in an insulting description about the Customer, which ended up printing onto the receipt that was then taped to the Customer's order, which eventually was seen by the Customer. On top of the insensitive insult the Customer incurred, think of how this would have played out over a decade ago, versus in today's world. Fifteen years ago this would have resulted in an angry Customer who would have never come back, and who would have told maybe a few dozen friends and family members about this horrific experience. Not today—the social media coverage this incident got was overwhelming, which resulted it in being picked up by major television networks. The negative PR this restaurant chain received was substantial. That is why it is so critical that organizations have strong Customer service training for every employee. Not just the new ones, but every employee on an ongoing basis. Increasing employees' Service Aptitude needs to be done daily, constantly priming your employees' minds of what world-class hospitality looks like, regardless of the industry you are in, be it the restaurant field, professional services, or manufacturing. Not to mention, a poor hire can cost you hundreds of thousands of dollars in negative publicity, especially with the power of social media today.

What is more important: Hiring, or training?

This topic is probably the oldest and biggest debate in Customer service. What is more important: How well you hire, or the training and culture you bring your new employees into? While both are very important, 75 percent is the Customer service training and service culture of your company. Do you really think that Disney has found and hired fifty thousand amazing service-minded people? There probably aren't fifty thousand people walking the earth who were born to serve. Companies like The Ritz-Carlton and Disney find good people and put them in such a strong service and training environment that doesn't allow for or accept anything less than excellence.

Attitude wars

In a blog post titled "The Truth About the War for Talent," author Seth Godin writes about how HR departments like to talk about engaging in a war for talent; however, it is really about finding good enough people at an acceptable rate of pay. What I like to call "reactively hiring anyone," or "hiring anyone with a pulse." Godin points out it shouldn't be a search for talent—but rather a search for attitude:

> There are a few jobs where straight up skills are all we ask for . . . What actually separates winners from losers isn't talent, it's attitude. And yes, we ought to be having a war for attitude . . . The best news is that attitude is a choice, and it's available to all. You can probably win the war for attitude with the people you've already got.[14]

The C in Customer

In the book *At Your Service*, author Frank Eliason discusses the importance of capitalizing the letter C in Customer. Eliason explains how every word you communicate is important. Words, and the way that they are presented, tend to play an important role in setting the tone. So he started to capitalize Customer to demonstrate their significance in the success of the organization.[15] I love this concept. It shows fanatical attention being placed on the Customer. I agree and think any organization that wants to deliver world-class Customer service needs to have that kind of attention to detail. Anywhere in your terminology, manuals, websites, advertising, or on social media, you should capitalize the word "Customer." You will notice in this book that the C in Customer is always capitalized.

The weather report challenge

I was working with a consulting client on the West Coast who has a large call center with Customer service reps handling their Customers via the phones. We were doing their Customer Experience Cycle workshop, and I referenced companies like American Express and Zappos as excellent case studies for great Customer support/call-center teams. As we were talking about how well trained Zappos employees are, I decided to do something I have never done before in a presentation, and I took a huge risk. Right there, on the spot, in front of the entire audience, I decided to call Zappos, which is in Las Vegas. I plugged the speaker cord into my phone audio port for everyone to hear the conversation. I received this very warm greeting: "Thank you for calling Zappos. This is Annetta. How may I help you?" So I said, "Hi, Annetta. I am leaving for San Francisco and I was wondering if you could tell me what the weather is there right now, so I know how to pack." Without any hesitation, Annetta responded, "Let me look up the five-day forecast for you. You know it is always cool there." You should have seen my audience's faces in total disbelief! Annetta shared with me (and the group) the five-day forecast for San Francisco. And I thanked her, and she of course ended the call with, "My pleasure. Is there anything else I can do for you?" The group was blown away.

I cannot stress enough that the quality of your Customer service is based on the Service Aptitude level of every single employee. It is the culture they have been hired into. It is the training they get from the interview process, through orientation, to everyday advertising, teaching them that no request is too ridiculous. It is the burden of the superior-service culture placed upon their shoulders that is reinforced every day. I have always said that the Ritz-Carlton has employees who are providing amazing service, and a year ago, that same employee may have been only providing subpar service someplace else they were working.

Blame it on the youth

Due to the fact that technology has dramatically reduced face-to-face interaction, the younger generation has fewer inherent people skills than previous generations, which ultimately means lower Service Aptitude. As a result, managers and companies complain about how difficult it is to employ this new workforce, a workforce often blamed for why their companies deliver such poor Customer service.

My experience has been the opposite, and it really goes against all conventional logic. First, I have found that, in my own two companies—The DiJulius Group and John Robert's Spa (150 team members)—and in numerous world-class Customer service companies, a large percentage of frontline employees fall into the eighteen to twenty-five age range. Yet this same group of employees, employed at these excellent companies, delivers outstanding Customer service consistently! In many cases, the younger generation is better at delivering genuine hospitality than the previous generations, who grew up with less technology and therefore had more face-to-face human interaction.

If the younger generation grows up with less face-to-face interaction and as a result has weaker people skills entering the workforce in their early twenties, then how is it possible that certain ones become world-class in Customer service? One theory is that there has been such innate interactive deficiency that once they get it, they love it and thirst for it. The younger generation is hungry for hospitality. It also comes down to their Service Aptitude training. Think about this: If today's younger generation lacks the skills gained from human interactions, who is responsible for improving their people skills and increasing their Service Aptitude? The businesses that hire them! We need to have better training programs, not just training on product knowledge and the technical side of the job, but also training on the soft skills. The companies that deliver world-class Customer service are the companies that understand this fact and provide training in Customer service skills. The second theory is about how well companies like Zappos, Chick-fil-A, John Robert's Spa, Nordstrom, The Ritz-Carlton, and Disney make their frontline employees part of a bigger purpose in which they play a major role. This is why each of those companies has young, fully engaged team members.

NEGATIVE CUES

Build your company's Customer experience as if no Customer
has bad intentions.

One of the biggest contributors to the Customer service crisis is
management's paranoia that Customers are out to take advantage
of them. This leads to a significant amount of time that companies
spend on creating and enforcing policy versus creating positive Customer experiences. Why do so many companies' agreements and
policies sound so angry? You should be friendly to your Customer
in every way you communicate with them.

Negative cues

Your Customers experience your brand in so many different ways.
It is not only the way your employees interact with your Customers,
but it's all the messages being sent to your Customers in countless
ways. It is imperative you take a step back and review any negative
cues that are making your business appear less than world-class.

Negative cues are everywhere! They are messages that businesses create that have negative language, that warn Customers,
and that are intended for 2 percent of their Customer base but

end up insulting 100 percent. Negative cues come in many ways: signage displayed inside our businesses and outside our buildings; on our websites; in contracts, agreements, and disclaimers; in spoken language and wording we use; in the physical actions of our employees and the way we dress; and basically anything that the Customer can see or hear. The vast majority of the time, you can say the same thing, but by rewording it you can make it sound like you are caring instead of threatening. Every interaction is a branding opportunity to articulate your genuine hospitality.

Verbal negative cues

Medical practices are the leaders in negative cues of all kinds. I have checked in for a doctor's appointment and the receptionist has said, "We need to *verify* your information." "Verify" makes me feel like they don't believe who I am, that maybe I am trying to use someone else's insurance information. Simply saying "May we update your information" works so much better and accomplishes the same thing. Another example is when a patient is being seen by a doctor and a nurse comes into the room during the exam and says "Your ten thirty is here" or "You have a call on line two." At that point, the patient is convinced the doctor is now rushing and more concerned with the patient who is waiting. Some great medical practices have created both verbal and nonverbal codes to inform the doctor without the patient realizing.

When we started John Robert's Spa in 1993, we immediately started calling our guests the day before to remind them of their appointments. To our surprise, some of our guests would be offended with these calls because they felt we were insinuating that they were disorganized and did not keep track of their schedules. That is when we made the slight change of wording from "reminding calls" to "confirmation calls." We have never had a complaint about a confirmation call.

Don't punish 100 percent of your Customers,
or potential Customers, for what you are
afraid 2 percent might try to do.

Signage

Signage has by far the highest occurrence of negative cues. I have taken so many pictures over the years of crazy negative signs I've come across. What businesses put on signs amazes me. Let's start with the most common negative signage we all see too often: "We charge $20 for all returned checks" and "We are not responsible for lost or stolen merchandise."

"Employees must wash hands before returning to work"

The "Employees must wash hands" sign appears in the restrooms of restaurants that Customers use. This freaks me out, and I think, *You mean they might not?* There was one fast food place I stopped at and before I ordered, I used their restroom, only to find that they had four of these signs up. One above the sink, one above the soap dispenser, one above the paper-towel dispenser, and one on the inside of the door. This made me think that this establishment must have a real employee-sanitation problem if they needed to decorate the entire bathroom with these signs. I chose to eat somewhere else. Now, I do understand that posting this sign is a requirement for most restaurants, but everything can be reworded. I saw a sign in a restroom of a restaurant that said it this way: "Cleanliness is important to us. We wash our hands before leaving." This is so much better.

"We reserve the right to refuse service to anyone"

Sadly, the message "We reserve the right to refuse service to anyone" is so popular that Amazon actually sells this sign! I had someone send me a picture of a sign that says "No English, No Service," which was posted on the business's door. Business must be really good at that place to blatantly discriminate.

Two distinctly opposite approaches to Customer service

On the register of one retailer, I read a sign that said, "We will not wait on you if you are on your cell phone while at the counter." Obviously, the business that displays this sign is frustrated and wants to teach their rude and inconsiderate Customers a lesson; thus, making them ex-Customers. However, Brian Olson, owner of 45th Avenue Cleaners in Portland, Oregon, has taken a totally different approach to Customers on their cell phones. He displays a notepad on his counter that reads "Don't Hang Up!" and allows people to drop off their clothes while conveniently jotting down their names and any special cleaning instructions without interrupting any important calls. Customers on their cell phones are a fact of life today. He has found a way to put a positive spin on it. Instead of punishing his Customers, he created a system that does not ruin their productivity, while respecting and keeping the Customer happy and keeping them *Customers*!

Nine no's on the door

I was speaking in Fort Worth, Texas, and stopped at one of those beautiful outdoor-lifestyle shopping centers, with all the upscale retail stores. I walked by what appeared to be a high-end wine bar, which looked very fancy inside. However, when I got to the door, I was shocked to see a sign on the door that listed nine things you could not be wearing, along with the recommended attire, in order to enter:

- no athletic pants, shirts, or shoes

- no hats

- no excessive jewelry

- no baggy clothes

- no T-Shirts

- no muscle shirts

- no ripped, torn, or frayed clothing

- business casual or business attire is suggested

Wow! Considering the affluent area this shopping center was in, I am not sure what this business was worried about. All this business needed on the door was the last line: "Business casual or business attire is suggested." By the way, I went back to the same shopping center about a year later and that space was vacant and for lease. Big shocker—I think the business owner was focused on the wrong things.

"Please wait to be seated"

Typically, you see a sign at the entrance of many restaurants that reads, "Please wait to be seated." However, one time I walked into a restaurant where I was startled to see a positive cue: "It would be our pleasure to seat you." Just the slight tweaking of the message can have a dramatic impact on the hospitable mood your business is setting for your Customer.

"Conditions of entry"

I was speaking to a large group of various business owners in Sydney, Australia, where a partner of one of the largest real estate companies approached me during a break. Just before the break, I shared my "negative cue" examples. The partner shamefully confessed that his company was guilty of some negative cues. When it holds an open house for potential buyers, it displays a sign on the front door of the house that reads "Conditions of entry" and it proceeds to tell you that you cannot enter with food, drink, shoes, or unaccompanied children, along with a slew of other barriers to viewing the house. I was so excited when this gentleman showed me how he had already started rephrasing this sign on his notepad, which read, "Out of respect for the homeowner, we appreciate you removing your shoes . . ." He got it!

No Customers allowed past this point

The truck-repair service center of TravelCenters of America had a sign, "No drivers allowed past this point," posted on the door that separated the area where the drivers waited and where their trucks were being serviced. While this policy was needed for insurance reasons, TravelCenters realized it needed to be stated in a better way. It now says, "For your safety, if you need anything from your truck, one of our team members would be happy to assist you."

Don't even think about it

On a trip to beautiful Cape Cod, my family and I pulled into an antique store looking for a parking spot and noticed a vacant space right out front. As we got closer, we saw a sign at the front of that vacant space that read, "Don't even think of parking here." That sign also told me that was not a place I wanted to do business with.

"Sales Guy"

A title is important. It informs the Customer of what your intention is—to benefit either them, or yourself and your company. What do you think of when you hear the titles "sales" or "salesman," "VP of sales," "sales associate," or the "sales department"? I personally think of a person or group that is out to sell me, out to make a commission. To me, it is a negative connotation representing a hidden agenda. I am still in shock today that so many companies and service professionals still use the word "sales" in their titles. Even the title "business development" puts the emphasis more on the company's goals than what is in the best interest of the Customers. I prefer account executive, service specialist, product consultant, service adviser. I had someone sending me a quote via email for insurance, and underneath his name was the title "Sales Guy." That really didn't make me want to do business with him.

Location, location, location

While I was shopping at the Apple store and waiting for them to get my new computer ready for me to take home, I asked the Apple associate where the nearest public restroom was. She responded, "Actually, you can use the restroom at the smoothie place right next door." So I ran next door and used its restroom. After I completed my Apple purchase, I came right back to the smoothie place and ordered my lunch and a smoothie. As I was eating there, I asked if the owner was available. When he came out to my table, I thanked him for allowing people to use his restroom. As I said this, his face changed to agitated. He said, "Did they tell you at Apple that you could use our restroom? Our restrooms are only for our paying Customers." I said, "But I didn't even know your business existed until I ran in here to use the bathroom, and as a result I purchased my lunch here." He responded, "Well, we have been here for nine years." Which was my point exactly.

This business owner totally doesn't get it. The entire reason you pay such high rent to be next to an Apple store is for increased awareness through foot traffic outside your door. The only thing better than foot traffic outside your storefront is foot traffic inside your store. I would take it one step further; I would give free smoothies to the Apple associates who tell their Customers to use my restrooms. Drive traffic through my doors! Businesses need to stop worrying about being taken advantage of and take advantage of opportunities to increase their brand awareness and demonstrate their friendliness.

Give it and people will come

Here is a completely opposite approach and an example of a business owner who gets it. In 2003, Jeff and Bill Smith (brothers) opened Easy Money, a payday and check-cashing financial institution headquartered in Birmingham, Alabama. Payday loan centers typically offer high-interest-rate loans and serve Customers who may have fallen on hard times, who need cash fast, but who are extremely limited in their options. Almost from the start, the Smith brothers did something totally unconventional, something you will think is crazy when you hear it. In each Easy Money location, the brothers put a Coke dispenser in the waiting area so Customers could enjoy a free Coke while they waited. This became popular with the Customers and popular with the neighborhood. When asked why they offered free Coke, Jeff Smith said, "We wanted to get our name out there in the community; we wanted a way to connect with local people. We became known as the place that gives away free drinks." Easy Money would also tell its Customers who paid off their loans to stop by, say hello, and have a free Coke.

This is where it gets interesting. People started coming into Easy Money for a Coke, often only for Coke, without doing any business. At first, this made the branch managers concerned they were being taken advantage of. "Managers would be calling me all the time saying, 'People are asking if they can have more than one.' And I would tell the managers to tell them to take as many as they wanted," said Smith. "Then a manager would call and say a woman pulled up to the store and her kids ran in and grabbed some

Cokes and ran out. I would say that is totally okay. More and more people are becoming aware of us, and we are training them who we are, where we are located, and to come in. Don't worry about how many Cokes people are taking. Most people are skeptical about walking into a payday loan center. This humanized Easy Money to the neighborhood." *Wow*, you have to love Jeff Smith's philosophy.

Worth every drop

Easy Money gave away so much Coke that the Smiths were earning trips that were only for Coke's top Customers. Easy Money gave away approximately two million drinks per year! This nice sentiment became a $400,000 expense on the company's P&L. Even I was blown away by this expense. I asked Jeff if he ever thought about stopping the free Cokes and adding $400,000 to his bottom-line profit. Jeff said, "No way. I can't measure the goodwill and foot traffic we get, as well as being an integral part of the community."

How did this work out? Easy Money's revenues grew on average between 80 and 100 percent every single year. They went from four employees and two locations to over two hundred and fifty employees and twenty-one locations before selling the business for a sizeable gain.

Restaurant sends consumer a bill for using restroom

This story is too crazy to make up. The Flood Zone restaurant, near Houston, Texas, sent a woman a bill for five dollars after she used the restaurant's restroom and left without purchasing anything. She was not a paying Customer. The owner recorded the woman's license plate number as she left the parking lot, and then had the local sheriff run her plates so the owner could get her personal information. For some reason, the sheriff complied, which is an entirely different story. Then, the owner took the time to sit down and write a handwritten letter asking for five dollars, and mailed it to this woman. Besides this being one of the worst Customer service examples ever, the amount of resources this owner used to track the Customer down is ridiculous. I am thinking the owner of the restaurant needs to be spending his time on other parts of his business than this (not to mention the sheriff).[16]

Store charges Customers "just looking" fee

A store has had it with Customers walking around the store without buying anything. As a result, they posted a sign informing shoppers of a new "just looking" fee at a specialty food store in Brisbane, Australia. The fee is five dollars and is nonrefundable if they do not purchase anything. It can be applied toward the purchase of products. They appear to be begging to go out of business. This is one of the worst policies I have ever heard of. No business makes it very long treating Customers like this. If people are not buying from you, you need to figure out why; is it price, product, or service? Then fix it—don't punish the Customer.[17]

LA restaurant tweets Customers' names that "no-show"

A Beverly Hills restaurant publicly shamed people who "no-showed" for reservations by tweeting and Facebooking the names of offending Customers. Red Medicine tweeted the full names of people who failed to show for their reservation:

> Hi Kyle Anderson (323), I hope you enjoyed your gf's bday
> and the flowers that you didn't bring when you no-showed
> for your 8:15 res. Thanks.

The restaurant manager defended this approach. "Invariably, the assholes who decide to no-show, or cancel twenty minutes before their reservation . . . ruin restaurants (as a whole) for the people who make a reservation and do their best to honor it."[18] While it is frustrating to have Customers who "no-show" prime appointments and lose sales as a result, shaming your Customers is not the answer.

Restaurant refuses to allow boy to call 9-1-1

A young boy had an asthma attack in a location of a large restaurant chain in London, Ontario. He asked store employees if he could call 9-1-1 for an ambulance, but he was refused by the restaurant staff. Why and how could such poor judgment be made? The employees say because of company protocol, Customers are not allowed to use the store phone under any circumstances. The employee did tell the boy that there was a pay phone across the street. Thankfully, another patron in the restaurant saw what was going on and used her phone to dial 9-1-1. To make matters even worse, reports are that when paramedics finally arrived, the restaurant's employees wouldn't let them come through an exit-only door. The restaurant chain said it would use this incident as an opportunity to teach emergency-response protocol to staff.[19]

Sheer madness

I have always been a fan of Lululemon, both as a consultant and as a Customer. For years, Lululemon was a case study for retailing excellence, creating an excellent Customer experience in its stores. However, 2013 was not a good year for the Canadian-based athletic-apparel company. Lululemon became the punch line of many jokes as a result of extremely poor judgment in how it handled the recall of yoga pants. As is typical today, the situation went viral on social media. You see, when women came back to the store to return the too-sheer yoga pants, the Customers were asked to try on the pants and bend over in front of sales associates, who would assess them before a return was permitted.[20]

Unfortunately, it didn't stop there. The secret to meltdown survival is to minimize the downturn. As if this approach wasn't bad enough, amid all the criticism the company received for these mishaps, it issued a press release to the media stating that continued complaints of sheer yoga pants are caused by Customers who are wearing pants that are too small! This was posted in the frequently-asked-questions section of its website: "The problem may be that guests don't have the benefit of doing an in-store fit session with one of our educators to make sure the fit is right for them." An irate blogger had this to say in reply:

> I find this statement completely idiotic, disgusting and unprofessional, and I really and truly feel Lululemon needs a new media management team that can effectively communicate publicly without insulting and alienating their entire customer base. What exactly is the point of a press release like this one other than to excuse themselves to their shareholders and, in effect, kissing away their loyal customers.[21]

Lululemon needed to fix its product and, more importantly, stop doing and saying ridiculous things. Making Customers bend over before returning pants, and insulting Customers by implying they are buying the wrong size just further hurts its brand. I am shocked that a company as good as Lululemon could put its foot in its mouth so badly. This is a brand I really believe in, and I hope the company will get back to what it does so well, instead of trying to cover up for its lack of "covering up."

Lessons learned

1. Remove "policy" from your employees' vocabulary. This has become such a big issue, a crutch that reduces employees' Service Aptitude and causes them to sometimes make horrible decisions because they are afraid of going against "company policy."

2. As a company, own up. Don't make excuses about why or how it happened. Just come out and say it was handled incorrectly, and that you will make sure it is never handled that way again.

3. Use your resources wisely. Focus on the right things and messages you enforce. What you are saying to your employees, Customers, and potential Customers sets the mind-set of what type of Customer experience your company is trying to deliver.

What negative cues can you eliminate or change to make them more positive?

There are many unnecessary rules, policies, and warnings that do not need to punish the vast majority for what a small percentage may try to get away with. For the following items, think of ways you can protect yourself but say it differently:

- web site
- verbiage
- terminology
- signage
- what Customers see
- agreements
- employees' actions.

5

DAY IN THE LIFE OF A CUSTOMER
Walking in the shoes of your Customers

Customer Empathy is an understanding of our Customers'
circumstances and finding a way to fulfill those needs.

World-class Customer service companies do two things better than
everyone else: (1) They dictate what Service Aptitude needs to be,
and (2) they make sure every employee walks in the shoes of their
Customers.

Think about the Customer experience your business provides.
How would you rate it? How would your employees rate it? How
would your Customers rate it? The next time you have a large group
of your employees together, ask them this question: How many of
you feel we provide a superior Customer experience? I have asked
this question hundreds of times. When the audience is made up primarily of one company, nearly every hand in that audience proudly
goes up. It is easier to count the hands that are not raised. Typically,
the vast majority of the group raises a hand, feeling quite confident
that they and their company provide excellent Customer service.

Then I share study after study, demonstrating how companies and their employees rank themselves higher in Customer satisfaction than their Customers rank them. Not a slight difference—a dramatic difference.

In the Customer perception business

Who's right? The Customer! Companies need to know that they are in the Customer perception business. Think about your own experiences as a Customer, just in the last week. How often do you experience exceptional Customer service, the kind of service where you want to share your experience with others and bring it back to work as an example of a superior approach? One out of every ten experiences? One out of every twenty experiences? The sad truth is that the majority of businesses rank their Customer service higher than their Customers rank it. Here is the million-dollar question: Why is there such a huge gap between what businesses think they provide in Customer experience and what their Customers think? You can spend hours on this question alone with your management teams, and the discussions and takeaways around this would be incredibly valuable.

Don't ask the Customer what they want;

give them what they can't live without.

When I ask, "Why do we (businesses/employees) feel we deliver Customer service so much better than the Customers rate us?" the two most common answers are (1) we don't ask our Customers what they want, and (2) our Customers all have different wants and needs. Let's look at both of these common answers.

"We don't ask our Customers what they want"

While learning from our Customers is critical to building the experience we deliver, many companies do a fairly good job measuring the Customers' satisfaction through their own devices or have outside companies collecting this data. I agree this needs to be done; however, on the flip side, you can't ask the Customer what they want; you have to give them what they can't live without. Think about all the companies that have revolutionized their industries, broken the old paradigm, and turned everything on its head: Zappos, Amazon, Starbucks, Southwest Airlines, and Apple. They didn't improve on what everyone else was doing; they completely transformed the way it was being done.

Let's pretend it's the 1970s and we got a small group of coffee drinkers together and asked them what they would like in a coffee-drinking experience. They would have looked at us as if we had two heads and would have said, "A coffee-drinking what? There are two ways to have your coffee: with or without cream, and without or without sugar, for twenty-five cents. What experience?" And they would have been right. Not one of them would have raised their hand and said, "I would like to be able to spend ten to twenty times as much." Or you wouldn't have heard, "I would like to be able to order it over eighty thousand different ways and get it." (You really can have your Starbucks made over eighty thousand ways). Someone else probably would not have said, "I would like to be able to hang out here for a couple of hours." You wouldn't have heard any of those ideas from Customer focus groups, which means we probably would not have ended up with Starbucks. Just the same way we wouldn't have ended up with the iPhone or Amazon. Customers can only think in terms of what they have previously experienced, and that is typically not revolutionary.

"Our Customers all have different wants and needs"
This may be true, too, that many of our Customers have different needs. But before we go and throw our hands up in the air and say we can't please everyone, remember that companies like the Ritz-Carlton, Amazon, and Chick-fil-A all have Customers with different needs as well. They have found a way to build an experience that consistently pleases the majority of their core Customers.

The million-dollar answer

Here is the real answer to why we (the business/employees) feel we deliver Customer service so much better than our Customers perceive: we are not in our Customers' shoes. We do not relate to their reality. We are not them and have never been them. A great example of this is one organization we worked with, a chain of nutritional-supplement retail stores. The chain's average employee is a male, around twenty-two years old, in amazing shape. Its average Customer is a female, between the ages of thirty-five and forty-five, trying to lose weight. How can a buff young man—who can hit the gym for a few hours a day—conceivably relate to a forty-year-old mom who has virtually no free time on her hands, and who is struggling to lose twenty pounds? And if you can't relate to someone else's situation or circumstances, it is impossible to have any kind of empathy for them. Without empathy, you lack compassion and creativity.

Life as a business traveler

I was consulting with a very large resort in Orlando, Florida, that derives the biggest portion of its revenue from conventions held on its property. Prior to one of my workshops with the guest-relations team (front desk, receptionists, concierges, etc.), I had done research with the guest-relations manager, asking for her to share any drawbacks or obstacles in the receptionist's job. One of the answers I received as an obstacle was "dealing with business travelers." While that answer surprised me, I was more curious about what was so difficult about dealing with business travelers, since I was one. When I dug a little deeper, she said things like "If you inconvenience them even twenty to thirty minutes, they can become extremely upset and irrational."

When I met with the entire guest-relations team (150+ employees), I asked them, "How many of you travel once a week?" No hands were raised. I then asked, "How many of you travel twice a month?" Not one person's hand went up. I then said to all of them, "So none of you know what it is like to be a typical business traveler each week, getting up at five a.m., rushing to the airport, waiting in line to get on a shuttle, to get a boarding pass, to get through security, to board a plane, to get off a plane, to get their luggage, and get a taxi. However, that business traveler expects that he will have all those waits and inconveniences. Now, the only thing that is keeping him from collapsing on a bed or making it to a meeting is this front-desk person who says, at three thirty in the afternoon, 'Sorry Mr. Smith, but your room is not ready.' And he gets upset and says, 'Did you not know I was coming?' "

I asked them, "What if you got to see this business traveler's day unfold on a reality TV show, and you see his day from the moment he gets up, all the way to the point when he gets out of the cab at your front door? And you saw all the waiting in lines and inconveniences he went through until he walked up in front of you at this counter? If you saw all of that, now would his room have been ready?" Some say yes, some say no. Truth is, probably not. Receptionists cannot control housekeeping, inventory, and late checkouts. But what would be different? They all answered, "How we handled the situation." Bingo! They may say, "Mr.

Jones, unfortunately your room is not ready. Can you tell me what it is that you need right now?" and he may answer with "I have a meeting in forty-five minutes with an important client and I need to shower and change." And the hotel employee can respond with "Well, Mr. Jones, we can help you. We have a men's spa, with all the amenities, showers, toiletries, and everything else that you will need. Can I show you there?" Problem solved!

How can we expect front-desk receptionists to have compassion and empathy if they can't relate to what their type of Customer goes through on a given day? Once they can appreciate what it is like to be that person, they can then be creative with problem-solving solutions to help their Customer instead of viewing them as just overly demanding people.

A day-in-the-life-of-a-Customer video

Today, the first place The DiJulius Group starts with our consulting clients is by helping them create a day-in-the-life-of-a-Customer video. Here is how it came to be. We were working with TravelCenters of America (TA), the largest full-service travel-center company in the United States, serving professional drivers and motorists alike. One of the first units I worked with was TA's truck-service center, which repairs the trucks for over-the-road truck drivers. Consider being an employee of TA, either a manager, technician working on the truck, or truck-service adviser (counter person at TA's truck-service center). All have to deal with dozens of demanding drivers coming in each day, upset that their truck is in need of repair and feeling that this is the last thing they needed to have happen to them. Driver after driver, hour after hour, day after day, you can see how easy it would be to become numb to every driver, all wanting you to take them first and get them back on the road immediately, regardless of how many other drivers came in ahead of them.

Understand their circumstances, their pain, and their needs

So, in a strategic planning meeting on how to change the culture, we had to change the employees' mind-set, had to find a way to get them to be more empathetic and compassionate to the Customers they are serving. It wouldn't be easy. It would take a strong awareness campaign to change their Service Aptitude and get them to understand the "plight of the driver." What is it like to be a driver for a day? What are their demands, their personal commitments to their families, their timeframes to return home, their professional commitments to their company, and the delivery deadlines of their Customers? How could TA impact all of that? I said, "Wouldn't it be cool if we could make a video of a day in the life of a driver?" That is when Ara Bagdasarian, executive vice president of truck services, saw how important this was and gave the green light and said, "Okay, let's do it!" And they did.

The day in the life of a driver

TravelCenters of America created an incredible training video titled *A Day in the Life of a Driver*. It depicted a typical day of a driver who has not been home or seen his family for an extended period of time. It shows all the demands he has personally and professionally. His goal is to make it home for his son's basketball game that evening. He hasn't seen his son play, and his son wants him at this game. He finds out that more and more drivers he works with are being laid off, which makes him concerned for his job. He finally makes all his stops and is headed home to see his son's game. Just then, one of his tires blows and he shouts, "Not now, not a tire!" And you hear his son's voice saying, "You've got to make it home tonight. You have to see me play." You realize he probably isn't going to see his son's game as a result of his flat tire. The last thing you see is the driver pulling into a TravelCenters of America truck-repair location. It is gripping. That is how a day-in-the-life-of-a-Customer video should end—like a cliff-hanger. What happens next? Hopefully, the right employee, who got to see this driver's day unfold, will be saying to his or her coworkers, "I got this one, I got this next driver coming in." They are going to be determined to help him get back on the road and home in time.

In the case of TravelCenters, that is every driver's situation. No matter what they have going on in their life, no one wants to have a truck break down and be late for the rest of their stops and have to work much later than they are supposed to. So it is realistic that nearly every driver walking in has that similar state of mind. TA needs its employees to empathize. Every one of the four thousand TravelCenter truck-service employees has seen the video, and every new hire watches it. It has had a major impact on how TA employees handle Customers. Employees no longer take a driver's frustration personally, and they realize that they have a unique opportunity to be a hero to nearly every Customer who comes in. Every one of their Customers is in need of help: someone to come to their rescue, saving their day. How many of us have the opportunity to be a hero to our Customers? TravelCenters has repositioned the employees' mind-set to *How can I be a hero today*? Who is going to put on the Superman cape and come to the rescue?

Captain QFORCE

One of the highest awards you can win at TA's annual awards is the Captain QFORCE bobblehead, which goes to the employees who truly demonstrate the spirit of coming to the rescue for their Customers on a regular basis. "The video had a major emotional impact on our frontline employees and managers. It really sensitized them and changed their perception and stereotypes of our Customer, the over-the-road professional truck driver," says Bagdasarian. "It put them emotionally in the shoes of our driver and made them realize how hard their job is and that they are fathers and mothers with family challenges just like them. Nearly all employees, including former drivers, had a tear in their eye after viewing this, and our service levels began to improve almost immediately." Not only has TA's employee Service Aptitude gone up dramatically, so has Travel-Center's driver-satisfaction score, employee morale, and sales; and they cannot keep up with all the Customer (driver) praise of "above and beyond" stories that continue to come in.

———

World-class service organizations teach their employees to view things from the Customer's perspective. Remember, many employees have never been their own Customer, have never needed the services and products their company provides, cannot comprehend what the Customer's mind-set is. Therefore, they do not relate well and find it difficult to empathize, be compassionate, and anticipate Customer needs.

Every person has a story

Possibly the best day-in-the-life-of-a-Customer video is Chick-fil-A's, called *Every Person Has a Story*. This video is one of the most powerful tools I have seen, helping every person who works at Chick-fil-A to know how important that person is in front of them or next to them. The video is only a few minutes long, but the message it provides is long lasting. It scans a typical Chick-fil-A dining room, where you see guests and associates interacting. Throughout, little bubbles appear over different people's heads which share their situations. Things like "Fired from his job and is worried how he will provide for his family." Another one reads, "He is now cancer free," and the one that gets people every time is the one where a beautiful little girl is walking to her table and a bubble appears over her head that reads, "Mom died during childbirth, and dad blames her." I have shown this video to over a couple hundred audiences, and every single time there are grown men bawling like little babies.

Think of how many people you come in contact with each day. Everyone, in every job, is guilty of going on autopilot from time to time and just serving Customers without truly being present. Now think about the amount of people a person working at Chick-fil-A can see during lunchtime in one day. It could literally be hundreds. Chick-fil-A made this video, not for a marketing tool for the public to see, but rather for internal use, so all Chick-fil-A associates can see this when they start at Chick-fil-A—so they don't look at their Customers as a "spicy chicken sandwich and a Diet Coke." The video ends with this powerful quote: "Every life has a story." Chick-fil-A's president, Dan Cathy, sums it up: "This video was created to remind us that everyone we interact with is a chance to create a remarkable experience."[22]

A day in the life of a John Robert's Spa guest

Another good example of a day-in-the-life-of-a-Customer video is the one made for John Robert's Spa. It shows a lady in her mid-thirties. From the moment she gets up in the morning, everything is a blur, coming at her at a hundred miles per hour; everything is in black and white. She is trying to get ready for work; getting her kids off to school; stuck in traffic; dealing with road construction, the demands of her job; and people wanting, asking for, and needing things from her. More of the same after work with her doing many errands, acting as a taxicab driver, and dropping her kids off at different activities. You can see the stress taking a toll on her face. She pulls into the John Robert's Spa parking lot, opens the door, and instantaneously everything changes: from fast, crazy, black and white, to slow, tranquil, and in color. Smiling people greet her, await her, are ready to pamper her. A few moments later, you see her walking out of the spa. As she opens the door, the outside world turns to black and white and warp speed, but not her—she is still in color, at a slow pace, as she walks back to get into her car, refreshed and rejuvenated. She is superwoman again!

The objective of a day-in-the-life-of-a-Customer script is for every employee to understand the critical part that both they and your business's services or products play in their Customers' daily lives. More importantly, it's about how we handle each interaction. So, every person in the organization, top to bottom, must understand that it is not merely about a transaction, order accuracy, our expertise, average ticket, or number of transactions. Rather, it is about being present with every Customer and truly understanding the impact we can have on their day, personally and professionally.

Speed of service up, friendly down

When done well, just by watching the day-in-the-life-of-a-Customer video, it is obvious what your company's Customer service vision statement is (for more on this, see chapter 6). Actually, the Customer service vision statement should be the theme of the script. Many of our clients do a great job in ending the video by introducing the Customer service vision statement and pillars. Take, for instance, RPM Pizza (the largest US franchisee of Domino's Pizza), which needed its day-in-the-life-of-a-Customer video to help launch its Customer service vision statement and help change the company's culture to a world-class hospitality culture.

In 2011, RPM Pizza made major improvements in its already best-in-class speed-of-delivery service by improving its percentage of on-time pizza deliveries by 17 percent. However, according to an independent third-party mystery-shopper survey, RPM Pizza ranked last among its major competitors in hospitality. In 2012,

RPM Pizza began a journey and relentlessly committed to be a world-class hospitality company.

SPEED VS. FRIENDLY SCORES

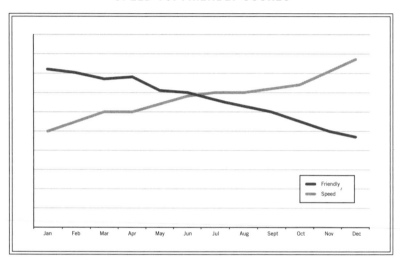

Think about the last time you ordered pizza to be delivered to your home. Why did you do that? It was critically important for RPM's employees to truly understand the "why" piece. Were their Customers hungry? Yes, but they could get food from thousands of places to satisfy their appetite. Why pizza, and why Domino's? This is where RPM's video, titled *Creating Smiles,* played a major role. To illustrate RPM's service vision, to really make it come to life and not just be another stale company quote, RPM's video needed to show all the benefits of what delivering great pizza in less than thirty minutes really provides to its Customers—beyond just filling their bellies. This video showed people being in a rush, with their busy lives, some away from home traveling, others trying to get home from work and get the family fed. In certain instances, it showed people trying to please everyone's tastes, wanting to spend more quality time with each of their loved ones instead of being in the kitchen preparing food.

It was vital that every team member understood that they were not just making and delivering pizza, but that their purpose—what their Customers truly needed from them—was easy and simple: Domino's pizza being brought to their door, exactly how they ordered it, promptly, by someone smiling with genuine hospitality. Thus, the Customers smiled because their lives were made easier. This ensured that every RPM team member clearly knew why his or her service vision was "Creating smiles by making lives easier." By 2013, RPM Pizza's service culture had made a drastic turnaround. Not only was its Customer-satisfaction score significantly better than the previous year, but it also hit the highest score in RPM Pizza's company history.

ULTIMATE QUESTION SCORE

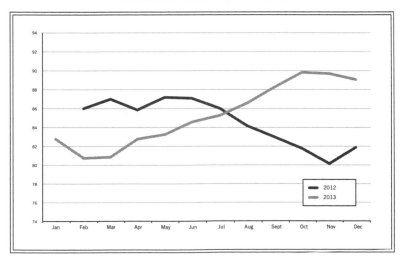

Changing your employees' perspective

The Maids International (TMI), based in Omaha, Nebraska, is a professional home-cleaning service with franchisee locations all over the United States. As it has been stated, it can be difficult for frontline employees to relate to their Customers' situations. Frontline employees often don't have the same socioeconomic status as their Customers. For example, you could see how a housecleaner working for a professional cleaning service could possibly be judgmental of a stay-at-home mom who lives in a half-million-dollar house. Maybe he or she would think, *This woman doesn't work and she needs a cleaning service?*

TMI created an incredible day-in-the-life-of-a-Customer video, demonstrating the demands that its Customers may have and how the employees who clean homes positively impact Customers' lives. Here's some of the narration from the video:

> What do you bring to the world? You bring hope . . . order . . . peace. You make lives better for the people you serve. For busy parents, overwhelmed by demands of family and jobs. For a widower who struggles with housework and looks forward to conversation and friendship. For an active mom longing for peace and order in a clean home. For a Customer with cancer who struggles to do even small tasks on her own. A lawyer away from home sixty hours a week serving low-income clients. A child with asthma who requires a dust-free home to breathe easier. Your work changes lives. *You* change lives. For all the people you help, we thank you. For all the lives you change, we thank you. You are the reason.

Who really is your Customer?

Ask your employees in every department who their true Customer is and you will get varying answers. Truth is, your primary Customer is the person you communicate with directly on a day-to-day basis and who is most affected by the work you do. In the business-to-business world, manufacturing, and corporate office settings, the Customer is mostly internal people who work at the same organization. Positions such as management, administration, IT, HR, marketing, regional sales managers, warehouse, branch managers, legal, and regional directors. Every single company I have ever worked with suffers from people in these positions truly not understanding who their Customers are, the person/group that is most dependent on their efforts.

*Your primary Customer is
whoever you communicate with and
who depends on you the most.*

While I was in college, I worked at United Parcel Service as a preloader, loading trucks in the middle of the night. I was never told that my Customer was the package driver who drove that truck I loaded, the one who had to deliver the packages all day. When I didn't do as good of a job as I could have, I would have drivers come in and share their frustration with me. I just blew them off as jerky coworkers. Then, after I graduated from college, I got promoted to a UPS driver and I realized that how successful I was every day was predicated on how well my truck was loaded and organized. Some days it was horrible; I would find packages at 3:00 p.m. in the back of my truck that I should have delivered at 10:00 a.m., when I was on the other side of town. Now I had to backtrack, making me late to all my stops and late getting home. UPS missed a golden opportunity to teach loaders who their real Customer was and how we impacted their day.

As I said before, in most businesses, frontline employees have never been their Customer, don't know what it is like to be in their shoes, and have little empathy and compassion for how what they do affects their Customer. As a result, today many of The DiJulius Group's consulting clients not only make a day-in-the-life-of-their-external-Customer video, but they also make a day-in-the-life-of-their-internal-Customer video, to drive home this exact point.

Create your own day-in-the-life-of-your-Customer script

Whether you actually shoot a video or just go through the exercise and end up with a slide show of pictures or have your staff role-play it, creating a day-in-the-life-of-a-Customer script will be one of the best exercises your company can do to change the mind-set and Service Aptitude of your entire organization. Ask your managers and employees to help you create, produce, and direct a three-minute video that would be a typical day in the life of your Customer. It will be a huge revelation. Remember, your day-in-the-life-of-your-Customer script should be like watching a reality TV show of your Customer's day unfolding. A roller coaster of twists and turns and surprises, both positive and challenging. As a result, your employees gain an abundance of compassion and empathy for every Customer with whom they interact. The script or video should not be about the actual experience that the business or the employees are providing, but rather it should be focused on two things:

1. What is happening in the Customer's life, prior to coming in contact with your business; their personal life, stresses, kids,

spouse, traffic, and their professional life, dealing with work demands, their own Customers, bosses, business demands.

2. How that relates to why and how they need your company's services and products, how what your company provides solves their problems or makes their day easier, better, or even helps make their dreams come true.

CUSTOMER SERVICE VISION STATEMENT

What gets your employees out of bed in the morning and rushing to work?

A revolution starts with a clear vision of a world different than the one we live in today.

—*SIMON SINEK*

The Customer service vision statement is most critical to employees

Most companies have multiple organizational statements—a mission, purpose, even a vision statement—but very few have a Customer service vision statement. The problem with having numerous statements is that employees can't keep track of them or remember them.

So why would a company want to consider adding another statement, a Customer service vision statement? The reason is that a Customer service vision statement is the one thing employees can control, influence, and impact. While mission statements are the corporate norm, they are more of a long-range goal. Take, for example, one company's mission statement: "to be the most respected financial institution in the world." What can employees do on a daily basis to affect that? Does that fire them up, get them racing to come to work? This is where a Customer service vision statement comes into play. If your employees are only going to remember one thing, one organizational statement, it should be your Customer service vision statement. A Customer service vision statement is not for anyone outside the organization to see. It is only to be marketed to your employees. A Customer service vision statement is this:

> The true underlying value of how your employees treat each
> and every Customer; a statement that provides a meaningful
> purpose to your employees.[23]

World-class Customer service companies have a strong Customer service vision statement. A service vision statement serves as a rallying point across the organization by being the one thing that all employees have in common, no matter what the individual job or title may be. It is how your business and the people who work in your business will make the world a better place. The right vision inspires team members and turns them into evangelists for the company. And a group of evangelists can change the world.[24]

You must start with a service vision before anything else can take shape in your organization. The service vision drives hiring, standards, and training, and it reflects leadership philosophies. All employees, regardless of their seniority, department, or title, need to understand how their positions and contributions impact the overall success of the company and its service vision. Without clearly drawing that connection, many times the vision becomes just another theme, slogan, flavor of the month, or management by best seller. A solid service vision is the foundation of the business; it should last for decades, as it represents what the company stands for, why it exists, and how all employees can play a part in that vision.[25]

A service vision represents the purpose of a company's existence, the heart of what it is at its core.

It's a Wonderful Life

The classic movie *It's a Wonderful Life*, written and directed by Frank Capra, is one of my all-time favorite movies. For those of you who haven't seen it, the premise of the storyline is about George Bailey (Jimmy Stewart), a man who has given up his dreams in order to help others and whose imminent suicide on Christmas Eve brings about the intervention of his guardian angel. Clarence, the angel, shows George all the lives he has touched and how different life in his community of Bedford Falls would be had he never been born. It is an amazing lesson on how much we can affect the world. I like to use this movie as an example when we discuss the impact a company can make on their Customers and community. What if your business was never created? Would your Customers still be able to purchase similar services and products elsewhere? Yes, but hopefully something would be significantly inferior if your business had not been in their lives or community.

Starbucks turnaround

One of the most amazing US business stories, the Starbucks Corporation, celebrated its fortieth year in business in 2012. On the occasion, Howard Schultz, Starbucks' chief executive officer, was interviewed by the *Wall Street Journal*. I was extremely impressed by how honest Schultz was about why the company started to decline a few years earlier, and what it had to do to get back on track. Here's Schultz:

> Putting our feet in the shoes of the Customers, [we understood] what they were dealing with and [their] anxiety . . . We were growing the company with such speed and aggression that we lost sight of the Customer experience.[26]

In 2010, I had one of the highlights of my consulting career: Starbucks asked me to help it re-create its Customer service vision statement. I have worked with Starbucks in the past, but this was different. I knew this was going to be something that would live for a long, long time in Starbucks. Starbucks has always been one of my favorite companies, both as a Customer and as a Customer service consultant. I was so excited! I knew that no one helped create better Customer service vision statements than The DiJulius Group. I knew we were perfect for this project. I was so excited about taking on this project, until I asked them what their current vision statement was that they wanted to change: "To inspire and nurture the human spirit one person, one cup, and one neighborhood at a time."

I thought to myself, *Wow, that's pretty good.* I honestly didn't know if we could improve on that. I asked Craig Russell, senior vice president of global coffee, why he felt that statement didn't work for Starbucks. He replied, "We love the statement; those are Howard's [Schultz's] words. It is more of our purpose. As far as a Customer service vision, it is too big, too aspirational. We want something that's actionable, trainable, measurable." As I thought about it, he was right. If someone comes in and orders a venti soy latte, and the barista gives it to them exactly how they ordered it, in ninety seconds, did the barista inspire or nurture their human spirit? Probably not. That is something that takes dozens and dozens of positive experiences. I believe Starbucks does that. But it doesn't happen one time.

So we did what we do with all our consulting clients when making a Customer service vision statement; we started with scripting a day in the life of a Starbucks Customer (see chapter 5 for the day-in-the-life discussion). A Starbucks Customer is easy to relate to. Virtually anyone reading this book can relate, whether you actually frequent Starbucks or not. Starbucks customers are people with discretionary income who are battling the hustle and bustle of their busy lives, trying to balance everything they have going on personally and professionally—people dealing with the daily grind that can wear us all down from time to time.

Inspired moments

One of the biggest takeaways from this workshop that the group of executives from Starbucks shared was that Starbucks can't change what's going to happen today to its Customers. Whether they get a flat tire on their way to work or they are irate because their package didn't arrive next-day air, as promised, what Starbucks can provide (and does provide very well) is an escape—if only for a few seconds in the Customer's day. Starbucks allows its Customers to step inside, collect themselves, see some friendly faces—whether it be the workers, friends, or neighbors from the community—and take a break, enjoy a beverage, regroup, and then go back and take on the world again.

There it was. The team had it: the Starbucks' Customer service vision statement. One of my proudest trophies as a consultant is the Starbucks green apron. The next time you walk into a Starbucks, anywhere in the world, and you see a Starbucks employee wearing that signature green apron, politely ask them to turn the inside top of the apron over for you. There is where you will see the Starbucks Customer service vision statement and pillars printed. It reads:

We create inspired moments in each customer's day.
ANTICIPATE CONNECT PERSONALIZE OWN

Why is the service vision statement printed on the inside of the green apron? It isn't for the Customers or public to see; it is for the Starbucks employees to see. And every time they put that apron over their head, they are reminded of their job for every Customer with whom they come in contact with.

The pillars to the Starbucks service vision statement
The four pillars to the Starbucks service vision statement have to do with the company's key drivers of Customer satisfaction:

- **Anticipate**—This might mean that if a barista notices a Customer in a business suit, at 6:05 a.m., ordering his coffee, while barely looking up from his smartphone, he probably has some place to be. Get him his drink and help him get on his way. On the other hand, it can be a completely different pace at 9:05 a.m., when a barista encounters a few mothers who just dropped their children off at school and seem to be in no rush.

- **Connect**—A connection could be recognizing regulars and having their drinks ready for them, or it could just be a smile or a kind word.

- **Personalize**—This means customization. With over eighty thousand ways someone can order a Starbucks beverage, you truly can have it your way.

- **Own**—Starbucks trusts its employees. They can own the experience. If a little girl drops her hot chocolate, a Starbucks employee can give her a new one for free.

Each of the pillars is critical, but only in conjunction with each other. Customers want their drinks made exactly how they ordered it, quickly—but not by someone with an attitude. Just the same, a Customer does not want someone to greet them by name and have their drink ready for them before they order it, only to have their drink made incorrectly.

> *People want to be part of something larger than themselves. They want to be part of something they are proud of, that they'll fight for, sacrifice for, that they trust.*
> *—Howard Schultz*[28]

The changes made a big difference for Starbucks. Earnings rose 44 percent, Customer visits rose by 5 percent, and more Customers were paying for higher-priced items.[27]

If you can't explain it in one sentence, it is not clear enough to you

My experience working with Starbucks made me think differently about a service vision. In my own companies, we had what we thought was an excellent service vision statement up until then. For seventeen years, the service vision for John Robert's Spa was "To enhance the quality of lives around us." I loved that; I was so proud of it. However, now I realized that it was too big, too aspirational for my JR team members. If a guest called and scheduled an appointment, did the call-center personnel enhance the quality of the Customer's life? Or, when our hostess checks a guest in upon arrival or checks her out after she receives a manicure, do we think it is possible to impact her life each time? Highly doubtful. It could happen over the course of many experiences, over a long period of time; however, it doesn't happen on a single interaction. So we moved that statement up to our purpose statement and worked on a new Customer service vision that a frontline team member could realistically understand and execute with each guest encounter. Similar to Starbucks, we realized we couldn't change what had happened or what was going to happen to the Customers, but we could help them get rejuvenated so they could return better prepared to take on the world as a result of their JR experience. While Starbucks typically only sees their Customers for a few minutes, we see them for a longer period of time, sometimes an hour or longer. John Robert's Spa's new service vision became "To be the best part of our guests' day."

One of the rules of thumb when creating a service vision statement is that it can't be too aspirational. When you first see that vision—"To be the best part of someone's day"—you may think that certainly it is too aspirational. However, if you think about the typical day in a Customer's life (see chapter 5), if a visit to the spa isn't the highlight of your typical day, we are doing something really wrong. We can measure it; it is actionable. On the phone, we want to be the best, most friendly phone call they have all day. When they enter the salon, we want their greeting to be the warmest, most sincere hello they get other than the one they get when their kids run into their arms when they get home.

201B and the 5:30 haircut

All businesses battle with going on autopilot and, from time to time, becoming numb to their Customers' conditions. While consulting with a large hospital, I found out that too often its nurses and doctors would refer to patients as "201B." Saying something like "201B needs their medicine." They were saying room 201, bed B, instead of the patient's name.

At John Robert's Spa, we are guilty of doing something very similar. Our service providers can look at their next guest as a "5:30 haircut." However, we have guests who ask their family members to purchase them a gift certificate to our spa for their birthday. After they get it, they request a day off from work, have it on their calendar, and are counting down the days until they can get away from work, relationships, kids, and all the other stresses in their lives. They look forward to coming into the one place where they can relax and be rejuvenated, so they can leave and continue giving to everyone in their world. I can't have my service providers looking at their next Customer as their 5:30 or their third-to-last appointment of the day, before they can go out or home. I need them to be present with each and every guest.

There is a myth that people who are more successful end up with higher self-esteem. It is totally the opposite: people with higher self-esteem become more successful.

The bounce

We get to give our guests the bounce in their step. This is why I like to tell my JR team members we have one of the coolest jobs in the world. We have the unique privilege, opportunity, and responsibility to have our guests leave John Robert's Spa feeling like they are a "10," whatever their "10" is physically, emotionally, and psychologically. When a person feels their absolute best, in every way, they have higher self-esteem. As a result of higher self-esteem, they are more likely to get the job, sale, promotion, date, or whatever it is they are going after. There is a myth that people who are more successful end up with higher self-esteem. It is totally the opposite: people with higher self-esteem become more successful. That is why we have an obligation to be the best part of each and every guest's day. When we do that, focus on that, they walk out with the bounce in their step, and we have just made price irrelevant.

To succeed in any business, you need an exceptionally clear vision. A vision is something you can say in a few words.

Feeling cared for unlike anywhere else you go

Chick-fil-A has revolutionized its industry by mastering hospitality unlike any other quick-service restaurant. Its story is remarkable. With more than 1,500 locations in the United States and more than forty years of double-digit growth, Chick-fil-A is one of the best case studies for Customer service consistency. Its service vision is "To make our guests feel cared for, unlike anywhere else." Make their guests feel cared for in a way that no one else does. I love that. They didn't say, "Make our guests feel cared for better than Burger King or McDonald's"; they said better than anywhere else Customers go. Chick-fil-A knows it is not only competing with other fast food restaurants. After you go to a Chick-fil-A restaurant, you don't then drive down the street to one of its competitors. You don't need to, but you do go other places, like running errands and dealing with other businesses.

Cared-for-meter

Chick-fil-A has a metaphoric "cared-for-meter" that it uses as a training example to demonstrate how much people need to feel cared for. Remember the Chick-fil-A *Every Person Has a Story* video (chapter 5)? It demonstrates all the different situations that are going on in its Customers' lives. Besides the personal situations, think about how often people experience subpar service in a day, constantly hearing things like "No, we can't do that" and "It's our policy." During any given day, a person's cared-for-meter could be around a three or a four (out of ten); then they walk into a Chick-fil-A restaurant and they are greeted with an enthusiastic smile, and they hear words like "certainly" and "my pleasure." All of a sudden their cared-for-meter spikes to a nine. Something significant happens to a person when they feel cared for. They may not realize it at the time, but they want that feeling again. They need that feeling again. A few days later someone is dying for a chicken sandwich from Chick-fil-A, but it just might not be only the sandwich that is drawing them back.

The Customer service vision package

The Customer service vision statement is the *what*. It should match the following criteria:

- Easy for all employees to relate to and understand.

- Simple, concise, and memorable.

- Actionable and empowering.

- Measurable, observable, and trainable.

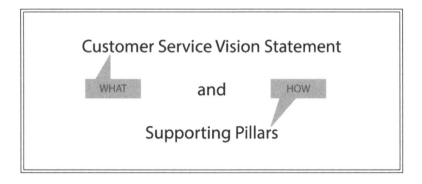

Supporting pillars

The supporting pillars are the *how* that everyone from your front-line employees to the CEO performs on a daily basis in each Customer interaction, and therefore executes the Customer service vision. There are traditionally three pillars that support the Customer service vision statement:

- **Pillar 1**—The quality/expertise of the service or product your employee is providing.

- **Pillar 2**—The Customer interaction; how we treat that person.

- **Pillar 3**—The autonomy needed for your employees to exceed the norm, do a little more, go "above and beyond."

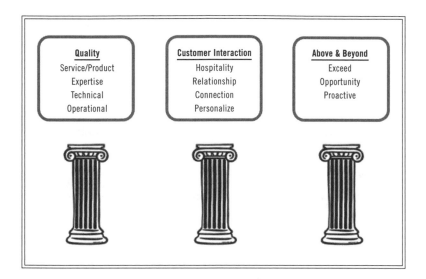

Quality	Customer Interaction	Above & Beyond
Service/Product	Hospitality	Exceed
Expertise	Relationship	Opportunity
Technical	Connection	Proactive
Operational	Personalize	

While the service vision statement is vital, I actually believe the pillars are even more important. Without the pillars, the service vision statement is just a statement. However, the pillars are the *how*. By executing the pillars every time, you can achieve the service vision statement.

The following are examples of The DiJulius Group clients' Customer service vision statements and supporting pillars. You will see each of the companies' service vision statements represent the three primary pillars: the quality/expertise pillar, the Customer interaction pillar, and the "above and beyond" pillar.

Restaurants Unlimited. Restaurants Unlimited, Inc. (RUI) is headquartered in Seattle and owns and operates twenty different brands in forty-six locations. RUI's service vision starts with executive sponsorship and high Service Aptitude at the top, which is exactly what the president and CEO, Chris Harter, demonstrates as well as any leader. RUI restaurants are extremely busy, and Harter and his management team want to make sure every team member treats each guest as an individual person by being present with each guest they come in contact with. That is why RUI's service vision statement is this:

"TO MAKE EVERY GUEST FEEL LIKE OUR ONLY ONE"
Make It Right ~ Make It Special ~ Make It Happen

Make It Right—About the quality of the food, perfect environment, attention to detail.

Make It Special—Connecting, sharing our passion, engaging, and making it memorable for each guest.

Make It Happen—Each employee is empowered to say yes, exceed, and find a way.

The DiJulius Group. TDG is a consulting firm based in Cleveland, Ohio, helping companies build world-class Customer service organizations. Here's TDG's service vision:

"TO BE THE BEST DECISION OUR CLIENTS MAKE"
Expertise ~ World-Class ~ Whatever/Whenever

Expertise—Be brilliant at service, provide resources and innovative solutions, anticipate needs.

World-Class—Build lasting relationships, create memorable experiences, utilize Secret Service.

Whatever/Whenever—Anything, any time, always *yes.*

The Maids International. TMI, based out of Omaha, Nebraska, is a professional home-cleaning service with franchise locations all over the United States and Canada. TMI's service vision:

"WOW EVERY CUSTOMER"
Deliver It ~ Personalize It ~ Own It

Deliver It—Be an expert, detailed and consistent.

Personalize It—Make it enjoyable, unique, and memorable.

Own It—Always anticipate, delight, and excel.

Superior Glove. This is a leading manufacturer and wholesale supplier of work and safety gloves, headquartered in Ontario, Canada. Its Customer service teams interact with its Customers, who are other businesses that use Superior's products—either to resell them or for use themselves—primarily over the phone and electronically. This is Superior Glove's service vision statement and its pillars:

"DELIVERING A SUPERIOR SERVICE EXPERIENCE"
Know It ~ Show It ~ Own It

Know It—Product knowledge, be accurate, consistent, and respond quickly.

Show It—Friendly, empathy, personalize, and committed.

Own It—Empowered, accountable, anticipate need, and fix it.

RPM Pizza. This is the largest US franchisee of Domino's Pizza, with 135 stores operating in three states with 2,800 team members. This is RPM's Customer service vision:

"CREATING SMILES BY MAKING LIVES EASIER"
Operational Excellence ~ Customer Delight ~ Deliver WOW

Operational Excellence—Perfect food, order accuracy, on time, and clean image.

Customer Delight—Make it positive, easy, personal, and fun.

Deliver WOW—Make their day, be a hero, and do something extra.

John Robert's Spa. This is a collection of upscale salons and spas in the Cleveland area and named one of the top twenty salons in the United States. JR Spa's Customer service vision and pillars:

"TO BE THE BEST PART OF OUR GUEST'S DAY"
Mastering ~ Emotional Connection ~ Give More

Mastering—Always improving, best trained and educated at our craft.

Emotional Connection—Utilizing Secret Service and Customer intelligence to personalize every guest's experience.

Give More—Surprise and delight; the answer's yes.

Advance Financial. This is a payday loan center, headquartered in Nashville, Tennessee. Its Customer base is often made up of people who have fallen on hard times. Advance Financial wants to make sure every one of its 500+ employees, in more than fifty locations, acts as an ally for its Customers. The company wants to create a place where its Customers can come in, be respected, see a friendly face, and be treated like a friend, hence Advance Financial's Customer service vision:

"FRIENDS HELPING FRIENDS"
Know ~ Show ~ Flow

Know—Knowledgeable, accurate, efficient, and consistent.

Show—Listen, understand, connect, and respect.

Flow—Anticipate, impact, exceed, and own.

Nemacolin Woodlands Resort. One of the dangers that can happen when you work at a huge hotel and resort that has people enjoying weddings, business conferences, and honeymoons is that you can think that a guest's satisfaction is based on how those grandiose events turn out. However, Nemacolin—located in Farmington, Pennsylvania—realizes it is not only about excellent food, the room being ready and clean, good spa service, and a beautiful wedding; rather, it is more the sum of dozens of individual moments that make up how guests will feel about their experience and the memories they will take with them. That is why Nemacolin's Customer service vision statement is:

"OWN EVERY MOMENT"
Be Excellent ~ Be Engaged ~ Be Empowered

Anytime Fitness. In 2014, Anytime Fitness was ranked number one by *Entrepreneur* magazine's annual "Franchise 500" list. Anytime Fitness is the world's largest and fastest-growing coed fitness club chain. It was also recently named one of "America's Most Promising Companies" by *Forbes* magazine, as well as the "Best Place to Work" by *Minnesota Business* magazine two years in a row. I haven't worked with too many companies that can rival the amazing culture created by cofounders Chuck Runyon and Dave Mortensen. Nearly 1,500 employees are sporting an Anytime Fitness logo tattoo. The purpose of Anytime Fitness is "to improve the self-esteem of the world." Anytime Fitness's Customer service vision statement is this:

"SURPRISINGLY PERSONABLE EXPERIENCE"
Care ~ Coach ~ Connect

The purpose motive

A service vision statement provides purpose to your frontline employees, which is critical for having high morale in a workplace. Daniel Pink, best-selling author and the leading expert on what motivates people, shares what he calls the "purpose motive":

> The companies that are flourishing . . . are animated by this purpose motive. Let me give you a couple of examples. Here's the founder of Skype. He says, "Our goal is to be disruptive but in the cause of making the world a better place." Pretty good purpose. Here's Steve Jobs: "I want to put a ding in the universe." All right? That's the kind of thing that might get you up in the morning and racing to go to work. So I think that we are purpose maximizers, not only profit maximizers . . . We can actually build organizations and work lives that make us better off . . . [and] that make our world a little better.[29]

Do not underestimate the power of a purpose

Why do some companies have a large percent of their workforce unmotivated and apathetic, while other excellent companies have the majority of their workforce willing to make ridiculous sacrifices in a cult-like culture of Customer satisfaction? Yes, one answer is that they select better candidates; however, I truly believe there is only a small fraction of people born with the "service DNA," the rest are grown by great companies and their strong, uncompromising cultures.

Think about the most selfless, most sacrificing people you have ever come across. I have found it to be anyone who has anything to do with the following groups: volunteers, charities, political campaigns, and student athletes. What do these groups and the people who make them up all have in common? They make little or no money, and in a lot of cases, it is highly unlikely they can ever make a living in any of these fields. However, they are part of a cause, part of something bigger. They are focused on their direct impact, and they have an abundance of pride and loyalty to their team. They are part of a special fraternity that they are willing to fight for. Now think of the great service businesses that have revolutionized stale industries with a completely new model, energized by a workforce on a mission with a promise to provide a truly unique experience. Think of a company like Zappos. It created the same sense of purpose that volunteer groups, charities, political campaigns, and scholastic sports have. However, it does one thing better: it pays its team members. A purpose and a paycheck.

Direct impact

When my middle son, Cal, was only eleven, he read a book about a politician and became a huge fan and supporter. He does not get his love for politics from me. During this time, he asked if he could work on this politician's Northeast Ohio campaign committee. I said I doubted they would allow a minor to work with them, but that didn't stop Cal! He called  and called and finally got the Northeast Ohio campaign director to meet with him to discuss how he could contribute. Shortly after, every night, my son Cal was attending meetings, making phone calls to registered voters, and knocking door to door. Did I mention that Cal was age eleven? The local newspaper even ran a story about Cal and how rare it is for a youth to have such passion and commitment to a political campaign.

The week leading up to the election, Cal wanted to stay up very late every night to make last-minute calls and knock on doors. I said absolutely not! I did not want him staying up way past his bedtime on school nights. Cal became so emotional and said to me, "Dad, you do not understand! The only way he [the candidate] will win is if I can do this. Please let me—I made a commitment!" This is coming from an eleven-year-old who has never met the politician personally. Of course I gave in; I couldn't turn down that type of passion and determination. His candidate ended up winning, and Cal is convinced he was the reason. But think about his sense of purpose, his commitment, and devotion for a cause—a vision. It is this type of purpose that I want every one of my employees to have toward our Customers and our Customer service vision statement. Now if I could just get Cal to understand the greater purpose of keeping his room clean and remembering to take out the garbage every Tuesday night.

Amazon founder and president Jeff Bezos is gifted at sharing his hugely infectious enthusiasm for his company. One of his incredible talents has been to convince employees, from the highest manager to the lowest Customer service rep stuck to her phone ten hours a day, that working at Amazon is not just a job—it is part of a visionary quest, something to give higher meaning to their lives.[30]

7

CUSTOMER BILL OF RIGHTS
Burden of the brand

You want Customer loyalty? Be brilliant at the basics.

World-class service companies have what I like to call a "Customer bill of rights" that every person in that organization clearly knows and follows 100 percent of the time. Would you ever expect to see a Disney cast member, in full uniform on break, chewing tobacco and spitting on the ground near the front entrance where guests are walking by? Doubtful. Or would you ever think a Ritz-Carlton employee, when asked for directions to the ballroom, would give a response like "I don't know, I work in housekeeping"? Highly unlikely! One of the most effective ways to elevate your company's Customer service level is by instituting your own Customer bill of rights.

"Never and always" list #1
If anyone is going to wear your uniform or name tag or represent your brand, you only need a small set (six to ten actions/standards) for your employees to live by. These non-negotiable standards are

also referred to as the "never and always" list. The critical importance is, if they do occur, you have to be confident enough that your employees recognize and understand your "never" and "always," and you can be confident that your employees would "never" do this and "always" do that instead.

If your company does nothing other than institute the "never and always" list and makes everyone aware of them, if your Customers rarely experience a "never" and consistently experience an "always," then you are in the top 5 percent of Customer service organizations! As you read through the list, you will see that they are all simple and common sense, but the majority of businesses and frontline employees too often execute the "never" list and don't consistently execute the "always" list.

In the examples shown, you will see that each one matches the following three criteria:

1. The items are typically one to three words in length.

2. They are black and white; there is no room for personal interpretation.

3. They are crystal clear and do not need any additional explanation.

Some things you wouldn't see on a "never and always" list are things such as "Always be professional" or "Always return calls promptly." Why? Because they are vague. What is professional to one is completely different to someone else. What is "promptly"? To one person it may be two hours; to another it may be two days.

The following are great examples of "never" and "always" items that are a collection from several great companies, and which The DiJulius Group helped to create. It is important to understand that these are not one company's "never and always" list. Ideally, you only want a maximum of ten "nevers" and ten "always." I have broken down the master list into small segments so I can share the logic behind them.

"Never and Always" List 1	
Never	**Always**
Point	Show them
Say no	Focus on what you can do
Say "no problem"	Say "certainly," "my pleasure," "absolutely," "I would be happy to"
Cold transfer	Warm transfer
Overshare	Take care of it

Point versus show

This is typically thought of in the hospitality business (e.g., showing someone to the restroom instead of pointing them there). However, in the business-to-business and call-center world, pointing happens all the time. For instance, it happens when we say things like "You can get that off our website" or "You need to call this person in this department." Why are we making the Customer do the work? We can send them the link, and we can transfer them to the correct department.

Saying no versus focusing on what you can do

Eliminate the word no from your company's vocabulary; no one should ever be allowed to use that word. You may not always be able to say yes, but offer alternatives and options and never allow anyone from your company to utter the word no. You will be amazed at how creative your team will get at satisfying Customers.

I never want a Customer of mine to tell me that someone from my organization said no to him or her. To me that is the worst swear word you can use in front of a Customer. While we cannot do everything our Customers request, we can always respond with what we can do. If someone asks if we can sell them something we don't even sell, we can answer with "While we do not carry product X, what we do carry is product Z, and the reason we do carry product Z is because it is proven to be the best, longest lasting, healthiest, whatever." By the time you are done explaining the benefits of product Z, that Customer should never want product X. If for some reason they still want product X, then you explain how and where they can get product X.

"No problem" is a big problem

The biggest street-slang terms used in every business today are the responses "no problem" or "not a problem." In fact, as a result of reading this right now, you will be shocked at how many times you will hear "no problem" over the next two days. Joe Schumacker wrote an excellent blog titled "No Problem, Big Problem" that articulates this point really well. "No problem" is a problem for two reasons. The first issue with saying "no problem" is that it consists of two negative words. We shouldn't be using any negative words, let alone two back-to-back.[31]

The second problem is that the "no problem" auto-response sends the message that what the Customer is asking of you is not a problem for you. However, when we are serving others, it is not about our convenience; it is about what the Customer wants. The phrase "no problem" places the staff member's comfort ahead of service to the Customer. Customers want to feel that their interests are first and foremost in the mind of the staff member, not that they may have inconvenienced a staff member by being a Customer.

Excellent responses instead of "no problem" are "certainly," "my pleasure," "I would be happy to," "consider it done," and "absolutely." Using "certainly" or "my pleasure" is so much more professional than the often heard "not a problem." It elevates the professionalism of your employees' terminology. It starts establishing a culture of hospitality where the Customer is first.

Cold transfer versus a warm transfer

Call twenty businesses today and ask to speak to someone, and nineteen times you will get a cold transfer—a receptionist who just transfers you to that person's extension and that's it. A warm transfer is when a Customer calls a business asking to speak to someone and the receptionist asks, "May I tell him who is calling?" Then she informs her coworker of the name of the Customer whom she is transferring. Her coworker picks up the phone and immediately says, "Hello, Susan, how are you?"

Overshare

Everyone loves to overshare. Why? Because they want to make sure the Customer knows it wasn't their fault. "I didn't know you were here." "The receptionist never informed me." "If I would have known, I would have been out sooner." Or "Shipping didn't next-day-air the package . . . I told them . . . I put it on the order . . . They do this type of stuff all the time." Does the Customer really need to know who screwed up and why? All they need to know is how sorry we are about what happened, and here is what we are going to do about it. If we need to address something internally with other departments or coworkers, that's our business. Our Customers do not need to know about our dirty laundry.

From the first "never and always" list, you should see how "never . . . *point, say no*, and *say 'no problem'*" each matches the three criteria: (1) only one to three words in length, (2) black and white, with no room for personal interpretation, and (3) crystal clear and doesn't need any additional explanation.

"Never and Always" List 2	
Never	Always
Say, "I don't know"	Say, "Let me find out"
Show frustration publicly	Be a duck
Accept "fine" or "okay"	Excellence is the standard
Make the Customer wrong	Make it right

Only saying "I don't know"

I am fine with someone saying "I don't know" or "I am not sure about that," as long as they follow up with "I would be happy to find out for you."

Showing frustration publicly

I want a bunch of ducks working for me. A duck is one of the most graceful, beautiful things gliding across the water, but what no one sees is it paddling like hell underneath. If something goes wrong, smile and address it, but don't panic in front of the Customer.

Accepting "fine" or "okay"

If you ask Customers how their experience was and they respond with "It was fine" or "It was okay," that is bad, really bad. "Fine" or "okay" means *Let me pay and get out of here and tell everyone I know why my experience with your business was not excellent.* Too many businesses don't train their employees to read Customers' faces and then address when a Customer is not happy. If someone isn't complaining, that doesn't mean they are happy. We need to dig deeper when we do not hear things like "It was excellent, amazing." When a Customer says "It was okay," your employee needs to ask, "What about your experience wasn't excellent? I would really like to know."

Make the Customer wrong

It doesn't matter whose mistake it was, even if the Customer is blaming us, we don't need to prove it to them. We just handle it and make it right.

"Never and Always" List 3*	
Never	Always
Forget you are on stage	Use Customer's name at least two times
Have a conversation with a coworker in front of a Customer that is unrelated to the Customer	Use your name at least two times
	Beat the greet
	Smile (it's part of the uniform)
	Ask, "Is there anything else I can do for you today?"
	Return voice mails the same day
*You will notice on the first two example lists, each of the "nevers" corresponded with the "always"—i.e., "Never point; always show them." In this list, the "never" list is independent of the "always" list. They have nothing to do with each other.	

"Never and always" list #3

Do your employees really know what is considered "on stage" and "off stage"? I have many retail-store and restaurant clients. After touring some of their locations, I saw some of their employees on break, standing in front of their location smoking where Customers were walking by. This is not the employees' fault. To them, they are on break and can do what they want. And even though they are not interacting with Customers while on break, if they are in uniform and visible to the Customers, they are still "on stage." This can apply to all our businesses: personal conversations being heard by Customers, nurses and receptionists chatting behind a desk where they still can be seen and heard, or an employee texting when they are in sight of Customers. Even if the employee is on break or has already punched out, the Customer doesn't know that; all they see are employees being unprofessional, not working, or not helping Customers. It leaves a very bad impression. It is management's responsibility to make sure all employees are aware of what is "on stage" versus what is "off stage."

Use the Customer's name and your name at least two times

In businesses where you get the Customers' names and reservations, check them in and take their orders, or answer or transfer their calls, every employee should incorporate the Customer's name at least two times during the interaction. The easiest opportunities to repeat the name? First, when you initially take the call: "How are you today, Mr. Thomas?" Second, when you are ending the inter-action: "Thank you, Mr. Thomas."

Just as critical is incorporating your name into the conversation. The more first names Customers know within a business, the more loyal they are to that business. Again, the easiest place for employees to use their names is on the front and back end of the interaction.

One of my favorite phone greetings is "Thank you for calling ABC, this is Alyssa, to whom do I have the pleasure of speaking?"

Say something positive

This can be a compliment—"Love your blouse" or "tie," "glasses," or "scarf"—or just a positive quip like "It was great to hear from you today" or "Enjoy your weekend!" Sometimes I get push back on this. Someone will say to me, "If you are encouraging your employees to say something nice to each Customer, isn't that a little unauthentic?" Not at all. What I am trying to do is get my employees not to be so "transaction focused" and be aware of things they should be noticing. There is always something nice you can say about everyone with whom you come into contact—always. Even if it's just a thirty-second conversation, find a personal or professional compliment you can deliver.

Beat the greet

No Customer should ever say hello, good-bye, or thank you to employees before the employees say those things. This not only applies to employees who are coming in direct contact with Customers but also applies any time an employee comes within ten feet of a Customer. They may just be walking by, but employees and managers need to smile, nod, and acknowledge the Customer.

A smile is part of the uniform

Another favorite of mine is a genuine smile. It's just as much a part of the uniform as anything else employees are required to wear: uniform, name tag, hat, and so on. Everyone should have a smile and it should be genuine. A smile shows teeth. In my companies, we have sent team members home for being "out of uniform," for not smiling. I like to tell my employees, "If you are happy, tell your face."

Is there anything else I can do for you?
I love this line, and it can be used in every single Customer interaction in every business. On the phone, face to face, checking someone out, via e-mail: "Is there anything else I can do for you today, Janet?" While an employee may have three other Customers waiting for help or forty emails in their inbox, just saying "Is there anything else I can do for you?" makes those Customers feel as if they are your only concern.

"Never and always" list for email

"Never and always" lists are just as critical for people who work jobs where they mostly communicate via email (e.g., corporate offices, internal support positions, and Customer service reps). Email has the ability to turn off the politeness gene in human beings.

EXAMPLE "ALWAYS AND NEVER" LISTS

The following are some examples from The DiJulius Group's consulting clients' "never and always" lists:

"Never and Always" List for Email	
Never	Always
Deliver bad/negative news via e-mail	Use a professional signature, even in replies and from your smartphone
Respond with just an answer (five words or fewer)	Use the Customer's name every time
Use jargon/slang	Open with something personal when dealing with an existing client
Treat email like a text message	Close with a nice line, e.g.: "It was a pleasure." "Looking forward to working with you." "Let me know if there is anything else I can do."
Use all caps	Respond within one business day (even if it is to let them know you don't have an answer yet)
"Reply to all" when the entire list doesn't need to know	Use clear subject-line wording
Get anything off your chest in an email	Use BCC when sending to a large list to protect others' email addresses
	Call them if your first email was not clear
	Call them directly if you cannot provide them with what they are asking for

The Maids International is a professional home-cleaning service with franchisee locations all over the United States and Canada.

The Maids International "Never and Always" List	
Never	**Always**
Say no	Say what you *can* do
Speak negatively or gossip	Be respectful
Criticize	Help everyone
Make excuses	Make it right
Hide mistakes	Assume you are on camera
Use profanity	Use a Customer's name
Show frustration publicly	Make eye contact/smile
Blame	Say hello, thank you, and good-bye

Restaurants Unlimited, headquartered in Seattle, owns and operates twenty different brands in forty-six locations.

Restaurants Unlimited "Never and Always" List	
Never	**Always**
Say no or "I don't know"	Offer what we can do
Point	Show them
Let them see you sweat	Be on stage
Hide behind policy	Find a solution
Make excuses	Do whatever it takes

Advance Financial is a payday loan center headquartered in Nashville, Tennessee.

Advance Financial "Never and Always" List	
Never	Always
Judge	Show respect
Show frustration	Smile
Overshare	Be on stage
Say "next"	Be welcoming
Say "they" or "their"	Say "we" and "our"
Say "I don't know"	Say, "Let me find out"
Hide mistakes	Fix it
Place blame	Own it

TLC Laser Vision is a national laser eye-surgery chain with more than fifty locations throughout the United States and Canada.

TLC Laser Vision "Never and Always" List	
Never	Always
Point	Show
Ignore (not greet the patient first)	Beat the greet
Cold transfers	Warm transfer all phone calls
Gossip	Be mindful of your communication around patients and other employees
Address our "Customers" without doing your homework	Anticipate and deliver our "Customer's" needs
Make excuses or criticize your team or competitors	Own it—even if it is not your fault
Show frustration publicly	Wear a smile
Use negative or slang words such as "not a problem," "I don't know," "uh-huh," "yep"	Use words like "certainly," "my pleasure," "absolutely"
Allow clutter in work areas or reception area	Maintain a clean and professional work environment
Show disinterest to our "Customer"	Greet patients by name, use their name often, and gather Secret Service information
Make our "Customer" *wrong*	Make our "Customer" *right*
Misrepresent the company	Wear TLC uniform and name tag
Be disrespectful	Be professional and polite
Say no	Do what it takes to make it right

The DiJulius Group

| The DiJulius Group "Never and Always" List ||
Never	Always
Point	Show them
Say no	Offer what you can do
Say "not a problem"	Say "certainly," "my pleasure," "absolutely"
Cold transfer	Warm transfer
Overshare	Take care of it
Say, "I don't know"	Find out
Show frustration publicly	Be a duck
Make excuses	Own it—even if it's not your fault
Deliver bad news via email	Make it right
Leave things to chance	Be prepared

The DiJulius Family—Like so much of Customer service, I have found that the "never and always" list also applies to personal life. The following is my own family's "never and always" list, which was created by my three sons, Johnni, Cal, and Bo.

The DiJulius Family "Never and Always" List	
Never	**Always**
Yell	Take others into consideration
Criticize	Do everything 110 percent
Argue with anger	Have fun
Be disrespectful	Say things positively, even when it is constructive advice
Make others feel guilty	Believe in each other
Put others down	Put family members first
Embarrass	Be grateful
Disrespect property	Show you care
Be a victim	Focus on FORD (family, occupation, recreation, dreams)
	Do right
	Do what you have to do before what you want to do

Banker's dozen

A great Customer service bank that I have worked with is Isabella Bank, with multiple locations throughout the state of Michigan. It has created a fantastic list of non-negotiable standards called the Banker's Dozen.

THE BANKER'S DOZEN CUSTOMER SERVICE STANDARDS

1. 10-4 Rule

When someone approaches within ten feet of you, acknowledge them with a nod and smile. At four feet say something—"Hello," "Good morning," "I'll be with you in a minute." Do it sincerely, from the heart. Smile.

2. You Had Me at Hello

Greet Customers, make eye contact, use their name, smile.

3. Don't Worry, Be Happy

Leave your problems at the door. Our Customers take their cues based off our behavior, positive outlook, and enthusiasm. Remember: "When you worry, your face will frown, and that will bring everybody down. Don't worry, be happy." Make the Customer's day. Smile.

4. You're on Stage

Dress professionally, act professionally, be professional. See yourself from the Customer's eyes. Use correct grammar. Be personable. Remember that you are on stage all of the time. Smile.

5. The Buddy System

Be proactive in identifying when your teammates need a helping hand, encouragement, or praise for a job well done. TEAM = Together Everyone Achieves More.

6. It's Five O'clock Somewhere

Follow up with internal/external Customers as soon as possible *or* before the end of your workday, whether you have an answer or not.

7. Use Your Ears

Ask not what your Customer can do for you but what you can do for your Customer. Ask questions; listen to your Customer's needs. Become a resource. Under promise and over deliver.

8. I Can Hear You Smile

Smile before answering the phone. Answer the phone within three rings. Identify yourself by name. Return voice mails and emails promptly. Remember to keep all voice mail and email messages current and pleasant.

9. The Buck Stops Here

Own the Customer's problem. Be helpful and go the extra mile even when it's not your specific job. Listen, apologize, and empathize. Take ownership of the problem, accept blame, and thank the Customer for bringing it to our attention.

10. R-E-S-P-E-C-T (Tell You What It Means to Me)

Treat internal/external Customers with respect and dignity. Use words that inspire confidence when communicating, such as "my pleasure," "absolutely," and "most certainly." Refrain from using negative terms such as "no problem," which may inspire doubt.

11. People Do Business with People

Know your Customers and their personalities, anticipate their needs, and treat them the way they want to be treated. Be familiar with the products and services that we offer.

12. Thank You, Thank You, Thank You

Say thank you to your Customers and to your coworkers. Customers' loyalty will increase with the number of times you sincerely thank them for banking with Isabella Bank.

13. Everything Speaks

First impressions regarding cleanliness and overall atmosphere of our buildings speak volumes about our bank. Let's take *pride* in our workplace.

———

Approach your interactions with your Customers as a relationship, not a transaction. Ask yourself, "What else can I do to WOW our Customers and go beyond the first thirteen Banker's Dozen.

———

One of the most effective ways to elevate your company's Customer service level is by instituting a "never and always" list of standards. If anyone is going to wear your uniform or name tag or represent your brand, there needs to be a small set of six to ten actions/standards that your employees live by. For consistency across your brand, you need to have confidence and trust in your entire organization, so that as these situations occur numerous times a day, your employees will never be seen or heard doing what is on the "never" list and will always execute what is on the "always" list.

8

SECRET SERVICE
Creating an emotional connection that drives ultimate
Customer loyalty

*If you are able to figure out how to be truly interested in
someone you meet, with the goal of building up a friendship
instead of trying to get something out of that person, the
funny thing is that almost always, something happens later
down the line that ends up benefiting either your business
or yourself personally. Stop trying to "network" in the
traditional business sense, and instead, just try and build
up the number and depth of your friendships, where the
friendship itself is its own reward.*

—TONY HSIEH, ZAPPOS FOUNDER AND PRESIDENT[32]

What is Secret Service?
Secret Service is not another term for good
Customer service, like going "above and
beyond" or "WOWing your Customers"
or "exceeding expectations." Secret Service fulfills a specific and necessary niche

in a company's Customer experience. Secret Service helps employees make a personal connection, which then creates an emotional
bond between the Customer and the company that transcends the
product or service offered. Secret Service systems allow employees
to engage the Customer, building rapport and relationships. Here's
the true definition of Secret Service:

> The ability to obtain Customer intelligence and utilize that
> to personalize the Customer's experience, leaving the Cus-
> tomer to ask, "How'd they do that, and how'd they know
> that?"[33]

Department of Customer intelligence

What is Customer intelligence? It is not how smart our Customers
are, but rather how smart we are about our Customers. It is Customer data (e.g., personal information, purchasing history, refer-
rals, personal preferences, home address, and workplace) that fuels
Secret Service.

Secret Service test

Which of the following scenarios *is* considered Secret Service:

1. Roses for every female client on Valentine's Day
2. Asking how a Customer's son is doing in college
3. Having an umbrella for any guest who needs one
4. Inquiring how a Customer's job at Progressive Insurance is going
5. A valet providing water in every car
6. Bringing your client a venti soy latte
7. Telling your client she has gained at least ten pounds since you have seen her last

While numbers one, three, and five are great Customer service actions, they are *not* Secret Service; there is nothing personal to the client about those actions. It is great that every woman gets a rose on Valentine's Day, but there is nothing personal about it. It is mass. Same with the valet putting a fresh water bottle in every car they bring back to a Customer. These are exceptional Customer service examples but are not personalized; they're not necessarily better, but they are totally different. If you chose numbers two, four, six, and seven as Secret Service, you were correct. However, I strongly encourage you not to use number seven with any of your clients. Secret Service is personalizing a Customer's experience.

Secret Service system implementation criteria

Secret Service systems should not add cost or complexity to your organization. Secret Service systems are what we call low-hanging fruit. When a company considers implementing Secret Service systems, they should first meet the following criteria:

1. **Low or no cost**—As you will see, nearly every example costs nothing but coaching your employees to pay attention.

2. **Simple to execute consistently**—Everyone's job is hard enough; we don't want to complicate or add any complexity to a person's workload.

3. **Has zero impact on productivity**—Secret Service should not add ten seconds to a phone call, appointment, or checkout.

4. **Creates an immediate WOW for the Customer**—More importantly, it is a pleasant surprise to the Customer that they won't get anywhere else.[34]

For all the promise of how social media
brings people together, still the most sincere,
lasting powers of human connection come
from looking directly into someone else's
eyes, with no screen in between.

You say you have relationships with your Customers . . . Prove it!

In today's world, the only thing that separates companies from offering just another commodity is the relationship they have with their Customers. If you do not have a relationship with your Customer, you better be the cheapest. Relationships builds trust, and trust is paramount in making price less relevant and giving any business a distinct advantage. Just because you recognize your Customer's face or know them by name does not mean you have a relationship. If you truly have a relationship with your Customer, employee, coworker, boss, neighbor, or anyone, then you should know two or more things regarding FORD about your Customer:

Family—Are they married, do they have kids, etc.?

Occupation—Where do they work, what's their title, what do they do?

Recreation—What are their hobbies, passions? What do they like to do with their free time?

Dreams—What are their short- and long-term goals, personally and professionally?

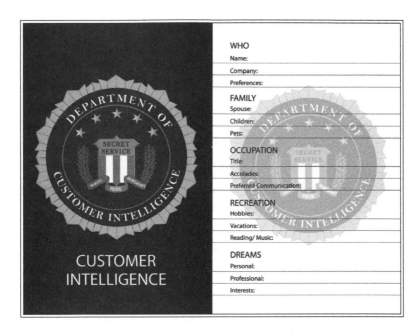

CUSTOMER INTELLIGENCE

WHO
Name:
Company:
Preferences:

FAMILY
Spouse:
Children:
Pets:

OCCUPATION
Title:
Accolades:
Preferred Communication:

RECREATION
Hobbies:
Vacations:
Reading/ Music:

DREAMS
Personal:
Professional:
Interests:

If you know two or more things about a Customer's family, occupation, recreation, and dreams, you really do have a relationship. FORD represents the things that people care about the most in their own world. They are the things they are passionate about, that make them light up when they are asked to discuss. Any time you touch a Customer via the phone, electronically, or face to face, you should be collecting and utilizing Customer intelligence. One of the best ways we have found to obtain Customer intelligence is through tools such as the Customer intelligence notepads and desk pads, as well as incorporating that information into CRM software that any employee can easily access.

These tools dramatically increase our awareness of all the Customer intelligence thrown at us each day, which we sometimes duck and dodge away from because we are too busy trying to execute the task at hand. For instance, Customer intelligence notepads are ideal for professionals on the run, in meetings, and at networking events. As soon as you walk away from the Customer, prospect, neighbor, stranger you just met, or anyone, write down key things they just told you (e.g., leaving for a vacation, alumni of Northwestern University, has daughter on a traveling soccer team). The Customer intelligence desk pads are for when you are at your desk, and it accomplishes the exact same thing, typically through phone and electronic communications. Then, when you have a moment later in the day, you enter this into your CRM system and are able to retrieve it the next time you are communicating with that person.

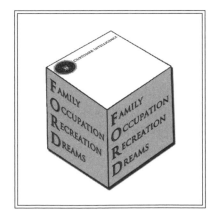

No time?

Collecting Customer intelligence is not meant to hamper your productivity. It is meant to enhance your listening and awareness skills, and it allows you to catch people's FORD. The DiJulius Group has a very large consulting client who hired us to work with its Customer service department, which handles inside sales and support for clients. Part of revamping its Customer experience was introducing Secret Service systems and rolling out Customer intelligence desk pads. We told their representatives not to do anything different on the call with their clients. We did not want them to ask any questions that were on the Customer intelligence pads (i.e., about their FORD). Given the amount of calls they handled per day, we didn't want to make them less productive, but rather more effective. All we asked them to do was write down anything on their Customer intelligence pads that their Customers shared regarding FORD. Within the first week of launching the Customer intelligence desk pads, one of the Customer service reps went into her supervisor's office and said, "I know Jim, from ABC company, was a plant for you today to see if I would record any of his Customer intelligence. He told me more today than he has told me in the five years we have been having a weekly call." Her boss responded, "I have not spoken to Jim or any of your Customers about our Customer intelligence pads."

The fact is, the Customer service rep heard more that day than she has ever heard before—because she was listening. For instance, when she said "Okay, Jim, I will talk to you next Wednesday," Jim responded with "No, that won't work. My family and I will be on vacation in Orlando all next week. It will have to be in two weeks." Bam! She heard it, she caught that, and instead of going into robotic processing mode, she was now able to capitalize on Jim's Customer intelligence. Now she can do one of several things: tell him to have a great vacation; follow up with him in two weeks and ask him about his vacation; or maybe, if he is a VIP Customer, she may say, "Orlando, that is great. At which property are you staying?" Then she can make sure to have some surprise (e.g., a fruit tray or bottle of wine) waiting in his hotel room upon his arrival in Orlando.

> *You need to show that you genuinely care about people first, to see Customers as individuals who have lives, and not just focus on the next Customer you are handling, processing, selling to, or supporting.*

It doesn't matter how you collect Customer intelligence. The critical piece is that you create a system that helps you pay more attention to hearing and obtaining your Customer's information so you can document and follow up, demonstrating that you are not like anyone else with whom they do business. That you genuinely care about them first as a person who has a life, and not just the next Customer you are handling, processing, selling to, or supporting. Personally, there are four things always with me: my wallet, car keys, cell phone, and Customer intelligence notepad. I don't leave home without it, so I can increase my awareness of FORD with everyone whom I come into contact.

Priming the mind for Customer intelligence

Did you ever buy a new car and were so excited because you had never seen your model in your chosen color, only to notice about a dozen of the same model and color while driving home from the dealership? Did a dozen other people purchase that same model and color like you today? No! They were always out there, but you

Secret Service

Collect and Use Secret Service Information

TLC Laser Eye Centers*

WOW
COMPASSIONATELY CHANGING LIVES

Name: _____

Nickname: _____

Birthday: _____

Scan Driver's License here

F

Family: _____

_____

_____

_____

O

Occupation: _____

_____

_____

_____

R

Recreation: _____

_____

_____

_____

D

Dreams: _____

_____

_____

_____

are just now noticing them. Your mind is primed to notice what it didn't previously. Priming is how we get our thoughts focused and directed to see things—new perceptions. Whatever your mind is thinking is what will be noticed. That is why Customer intelligence tools that you see constantly when interacting with Customers are excellent ways to prime employees' minds to notice and hear things they wouldn't have otherwise.

Moonwalking bear

To demonstrate the concept of priming, there is an excellent video on YouTube called "The Moonwalking Bear" that I love to show during my presentations. The video shows four people dressed in white and four people dressed in black. The narrator says, "This is an awareness test. How many passes does the team in white make?" And the viewer watches as the team in white keeps passing the ball back and forth. The narrator comes back on and says, "The answer is thirteen." Everyone is so proud that they got the number right, until the narrator then says, "But did you see the moonwalking bear?" And people in my audience mumble, "What . . . ?" Then they show the exact same video again, only this time you notice the bear moonwalking right in the middle of all the people passing the ball back and forth. And the video ends with this message: "It is easy to miss something you're not looking for."[35] No truer words have been spoken. Due to the emphasis placed solely on being productive, many employees miss glaring Customer intelligence that is right in front of their faces.

You can create your own awareness test for your employees. The DiJulius Group has done this for many of our clients. In each case, we ask the employees to focus on the task portion of their jobs. For example, in the fast food restaurant, we show a video of several Customers coming up to the counter to order food and drinks. We ask the person working behind the counter to tell us details such as what each Customer ordered and how they paid (cash or credit card). After they tell us those answers, we then ask them to tell us additional details about those Customers. The employees usually look puzzled. We then play the video again and show them several Customer intelligence things they missed the first time. For example, one Customer was wearing a name tag with their company logo displayed. Another Customer had a Hilton Head sweatshirt on. And when another Customer put her keys on the counter, you could see pictures of her children on her key chain.

Customer intelligence exists everywhere. If you visit someone's office, the walls normally display things such as college degrees, pictures of family, and vacations. The Maids International has trained its housekeepers to recognize the abundance of Customer intelligence opportunities they may come across. There may be a trophy or ribbon, which one of the children just won, on the kitchen counter of the home they are cleaning. The Maids like to leave thank-you cards after they are done cleaning the home, and in this case could include a note in the card saying, "We want to congratulate your son for doing so well in his swimming event."

Show me you care more about helping my
business than just getting my business.

Secret Service allowance

Benson Kearley IFG, headquartered in Toronto, Canada, is not your typical insurance agency, because Stephen Kearley is not your typical president of a company. BKIFG is obsessed with providing a world-class experience to both Customers and employees, and it is paying huge dividends with exponential growth. A few years ago, BKIFG started one of my favorite Secret Service systems, called the Secret Service Allowance program. This program provides every one of its business professionals a twenty-five dollar allowance that they must spend every month on their Customers, to surprise and delight them unexpectedly. This Secret Service allowance primes the mind for its employees to listen and catch opportunities to recognize Customers with soft, warm touches. For example, an existing Customer might just be calling to ask a question about their policy, and during the call they mention that it's their wedding anniversary this weekend, or they are taking their daughter to college. This may trigger the BKIFG employee to send flowers to one client. Other employees have sent five different Customers a five-dollar gift card to a local café.

Director of first impressions

In a professional office environment, when you might get fewer than a dozen scheduled visitors a day, a great and easy Secret Service system is displaying a sign welcoming people who have appointments today (e.g., "ABC would like to welcome Joanna Smith"). The DiJulius Group and several other companies have taken this concept to a new level with social media vehicles such as LinkedIn. Our welcome monitor doesn't just have our clients' names on it, but their pictures as well. This provides a unique experience for the visitor; it also educates the staff on who is coming in today, at what time, and what that person looks like, so they can recognize them by name.

Picture the traditional office visit experience: you have an appointment at your accountant's office or you are interviewing for a new job. You walk into the business and the receptionist says, "Can I help you?" You say, "Yes, I am here to see Mike Jones." The receptionist asks, "What's your name?" You tell her and she notifies the person, and eventually Mike comes out to get you.

Now imagine walking into an office for an appointment and you see a monitor that welcomes you by name and displays your picture. The receptionist says, "Hi, Joanna, it's nice to see you. Mike

is expecting you, so let me tell him you have arrived. Can I get you some coffee, tea, or water?" On top of that, two or three other people greet you by name as they walk by you.

Reverse Secret Service

At John Robert's Spa, we borrowed a best practice I learned from reading *The Innovation Secrets of Steve Jobs*, by Carmine Gallo. I came across an excellent initiative by the Westin Hotels, designed to encourage deeper relationships between hotel employees and guests. New employee name tags included this phrase: "My passion is _____." Westin executives said that the passion tags opened a dialogue between the company's staff and its guests, and when guests start talking, they are much more forthcoming about any issues that might concern them during their stay. A simple phrase on a name tag encourages guests to talk and engage, and find out similarities and common interests, thus helping to break down barriers and create emotional connections. This is reverse Secret Service, where clients learn and remember things about employees, and it helps start a conversation and connection for future visits. Another best practice I have seen is name tags that

say "In training" on them. This can really have an effect on a Customer's patience and understanding while the new employee is not yet up to full speed.

Silent cues and visual triggers

We need to use our eyes and ears to make decisions that enhance the Customer experience. What does it mean when a Customer is reading the menu posted on the wall at a café? There's a good chance it means this is a new Customer. Regular Customers of cafés or quick-service restaurants know exactly what they want; they don't ever look at the menu. A person standing at the front of a retail store scanning the aisles is not familiar with how the store is laid out. Two people engaged in an in-depth conversation at lunch, maybe an interview, would probably prefer not to have as many interruptions as someone sitting alone. Your training needs to help your employees be more aware as to what silent cues are being demonstrated by the Customer.

I am happy that more and more quick-service restaurants have started getting the Customer's name for their orders instead of just yelling out the order when the food is ready. However, so many are missing out on capitalizing on an easy Secret Service opportunity. After the Customer places the order, just before they are about to pay, the employee asks, "Can I have your name, please?" If they could just wait until after the Customer pays before asking for a name, they'd discover that 80 percent of the time, they wouldn't have to ask at all. Because 80 percent of the time, consumers pay with their credit card. They can capture the name from the credit card and then surprise the Customer by calling their name when their order is ready.

If you get it, use it

I love it when the first employee I encounter, be it on the phone or at the counter of a fast food restaurant, asks me for my name. However, what is so frustrating is that it isn't a successful system if the second employee, person I am transferred to, or the person bringing me my order at the table doesn't use my name. Otherwise, what was the point in getting the Customer's name?

Disney launches new Secret Service wristbands

How can an amusement park, which sees tens of thousands of guests daily, offer personalized service? Leave it to Disney to figure it out. The next time your family visits a Disney park, they may experience Goofy walking up and greeting your child by name. This is just one of the new experiences that Disney is capable of delivering as a result of their new trackable guest wristbands. Here's how the "Magic Bands" work: guests who opt to use the waterproof wristbands, which are embedded with computer chips, can then use those as their park-entry tickets, FastPasses, hotel room keys, and credit cards. Photographers can also use the system to link photos with the family account in order to buy and print out any photos of the group, should they choose to do so.[36]

Secret Service Anytime

The service vision of Anytime Fitness, the world's largest and fastest-growing coed fitness club chain, is "To Be Surprisingly Personable." If you think about it, "to be surprisingly personable" is identical to the Secret Service definition: "The ability to obtain Customer intelligence and utilize that to personalize the Customer's experience." To be able to do that with every Customer, every time,

Anytime Fitness had to create an incredible Secret Service system. A member uses a key fob (keyless entry device) to enter the Anytime Fitness facility, which triggers their information, such as their name and their picture, to pop up on their customer management software called Club Hub. The member's picture will stay up on the screen as long as they are working out in the club. So at any moment, a manager or team member can view a picture, name, and even some Customer intelligence of that member and then engage them by saying something to the effect, "Hey Jim, great to see you again. Third workout this week, great job."

Maître d' Secret Service

The maître d' at New York's Eleven Madison Park has created a fascinating way to provide Secret Service and make an emotional connection with guests. He Googles guests who have reservations at the restaurant, searching for Customer intelligence, such as where they are from, birth date, profession, anniversary, so he and his employees can personalize the experience from the moment the Customer walks through the door.

Collecting Customer intelligence from . . . Customers

With the rise of the social media era, Customers are more empowered than ever to have access to, and control information about themselves and their experiences. Some companies have decided to allow customers to access and edit their own account notes and preferences in the company's CRM system. The theory is Customers will provide better, more accurate information, which will allow Customer service reps to build stronger relationships when they interact with their Customers. This also shifts some of the database maintenance from the employee to customer, saving the company resources and time.

Every company is in the hospitality business

Here is the power of using Customer intelligence to not only save a big Customer but also to create a friend for life. The DiJulius Group was working with a consulting client, a large accounting firm trying to differentiate itself from all the other firms offering the exact same services. This organization can be guilty of having the old-paradigm mind-set that many professional service firms and their professionals can have. Often they have a stale, stubborn mentality that screams: *We are not in the hospitality industry. I am a professional who brings a highly valued skill set and intellectual capital that my clients desperately need.* Avoiding this type of thinking is the reason why the leaders of this accounting firm were launching the Client Xperience project, which was aimed at transforming their internal culture into a world-class hospitality company that just happened to have brilliant financial professionals, not the other way around.

Getting to "Benny"

About a year into the CX project, there was still a small percentage of the professional service providers, including partners, who had not totally bought in. At one of our regional workshops, one of the more influential partners (let's call him Larry) asked if he could share a story with the group. His story was about how one of the firm's largest long-term clients had recently changed its CEO. Any time an organization changes a CEO, all vendors are in danger of being replaced. So Larry went on to share that he knew he had to quickly demonstrate to the new CEO (let's call him Greg Benedict) how valuable and how brilliant the accounting firm was, before the CEO decided to start shopping accounting services to less expensive competitors. Larry admitted it was a struggle. Every meeting he had with Greg was short and very transactional. Every time Larry and his associates tried to make small talk, share advice, or demonstrate their expertise, Greg, who is known by his close friends as "Benny," was not interested in engaging in anything more than the facts. He just wanted bottom-line answers. Larry knew that once their current agreement expired, they were going to lose this large client.

That is when Larry started thinking about all the Client Xperience project training, systems, and tools they had been going through. He admitted that while he didn't put much stock in it, he had nothing to lose. So the first thing he did was figure out what Customer intelligence he had collected on the new CEO. He realized that there was very little he had learned in the few meetings they had. He remembered FORD (family, occupation, recreation, and dreams) and started doing some research online, via social media and Google. Through that, he discovered many interesting things about Greg, most notably that Greg ran marathons and was a big supporter of multiple sclerosis causes. At the end of their next meeting, Larry briefly asked Greg, "Is it true that you have run some marathons? It is on my bucket list, but it seems impossible." Larry explained, "Greg's eyes lit up like cannonballs! Next thing I knew, we were in his office and he was showing me pictures on his walls of different marathons he had run and was sharing experiences of how he couldn't even run one mile when he first started running. He told me that if he could do it, anyone could. Over the next few weeks, he was sending me advice, books, and articles on how to train. I also found out Greg has a daughter who suffers from multiple sclerosis, and that is why he is such a big supporter."

Larry says that six months later he ran his first marathon, with his new buddy and running mentor, Greg. Additionally, he has since become a supporter of the event Greg holds every year for MS. Larry went on to tell the group how Greg's company renewed its annual contract with Larry's firm, but best of all, Larry said that every note or email he gets from Greg is signed "Benny."

Secret Service voice mail

One of my favorite apps is YouMail, and it is free. It has many features, but the best one is the personalized voice mail greeting. Any time someone who is already in your contact list calls you, they will hear a personalized voice mail greeting. There are two ways this works: The first way—the simple way—is designed for the majority of the people in your contact list and allows you to choose a default recording that will insert the person's first name in the greeting (e.g., "Hi, Brian, John is unavailable right now, but will call you back as soon as he can.") The second way is designed for the people who call you the most (I did this with my three boys, key employees, close friends, and VIP clients). You can record a personal greeting just for them in twenty seconds using your own voice (e.g., "Hi, Derek, unfortunately I am unavailable right now, but I will call you back as soon as I can.") This app blows people's minds when they hear their name used in a voice mail system.

Mobile Secret Service

It is coming! Not only will cash be used significantly less, but your smartphone will also become the primary form of payment for many Customers. The *New York Times* reported that Square, a mobile payment app, will begin processing all credit- and debit-card transactions at Starbucks stores in the United States, and eventually Customers will be able to order a grande vanilla latte and charge it to their credit card simply by saying their name. This technology will eventually eliminate Customers from even needing to use phones for the transactions. This is crazy stuff! Initially, Starbucks Customers will need to show the merchant a bar code on their phone. But when Starbucks uses Square's full GPS technology, the Customer's phone will automatically notify the store that the Customer has entered, and the Customer's name and photo will pop up on the cashier's screen. The Customer will give the cashier his or her name, Starbucks will match the photo, and the payment will be complete.[37]

Who benefits from a personal connection?

Best-selling author Daniel Pink wrote a great blog about the power of making it personal. Pink tells the story of a study of radiologists in Israel. Their jobs were to read scans on computers. The radiologists were divided into two groups. The first group read scans as usual. The second group also read scans as usual, but they were given a photo of the patient for each scan. The latter group, those furnished with pictures, wrote longer, more meticulous reports. That was interesting, says Pink, but further into the study, it got really interesting. After a period of time, the researchers went back to the group who had been given the pictures of the patients and, without them being aware, had them read the same scans as before but without the pictures. The stunning finding was that about 80 percent of the previous findings were not reported! Make it personal.[38]

Think about that. The way most people think is, the Customer is the one that benefits when the employee makes a personal connection. But this example clearly shows that when the employees—in this case, the radiologists—have a personal connection to the Customer, they do a better, more thorough job.

9

RELATIONSHIP ECONOMY
Companies that teach employees to create relationships win

Today the only way a company can differentiate itself is through building relationships with people, employees, Customers, and the community. It is a new era, and people are starving for relationships like never before.

Want to see a teller? Pay for it

The banking industry has consistently been one of the worst industries at Customer service. To make matters worse, some banks want you to pay for face time, as more institutions are charging fees for interacting with a teller. It started with companies like Capital One 360, which was strictly an Internet-only transaction company. A Customer forfeits the in-person experience to save money, and if the app or website is down, the Customer's only option is to conduct business by mail. Now, other banks are getting into the game. Starting in December 2013, Customers with "virtual wallet" accounts at PNC Bank could see a monthly seven-dollar charge unless they pledge to bank only online, by mobile, or at an ATM. Customers

need to be able to interact with tellers; they are not ordering a book
or DVD. Banking products and services are extremely complicated
and technical. At Bank of America, Customers rejected "eBanking"
accounts that charged $8.95 monthly if a Customer used a teller,
which forced the bank to stop offering that service. While online
banking has grown significantly, the answer is not to charge people
to walk in your door and talk to your people.[39]

*The most important component to a
world-class experience is that the
staff isn't focused on selling stuff. It's
focused on building relationships and
trying to make people's lives better.*

Customer engagement is a contact sport

Don't just tell your employees to be present or to provide genuine hospitality, without telling them how. Make it black and white,
and make it measurable. One of my favorite hospitality systems for
making a Customer connection is the "5 E's."

1. Eye contact
2. Ear-to-ear smile
3. Enthusiastic greeting
4. Engage
5. Educate

Eye contact
This eliminates the head-down, uncaring, robotic feeling when the
frontline employee just asks, "Next." A great training method for

this is to audit the employees by periodically asking them, "What was the color of the Customer's eyes?"

Ear-to-ear smile

A smile is part of the uniform, and a smile has teeth. Demonstrate a positive attitude and let the Customers know that you are happy to serve them.

Enthusiastic greeting

Your greeting must demonstrate genuine warmth and not just a trained greeting. It should be one that shows enthusiasm in the voice, coupled with a smile and eye contact. We need to be giving genuine hospitality, as if the Customer was an old friend visiting our home.

Engage

Many companies provide little direction to employees on how to engage a Customer. This doesn't have to be a ten-minute conversation. Every single Customer can be engaged within the time it typically takes to serve them, be it ninety seconds in the fast food environment, two minutes on a phone call, or forty-five minutes in a meeting. This action demonstrates to the Customers that they are not a herd of cattle, or one of a hundred Customers. It eliminates being too task-focused on the *transaction* and replaces that approach with real *interaction*, which starts with using our names and our Customers' names. Utilize any Customer intelligence you can: find info in a database; recognize a name badge; point out a picture of their twins on the desk, a hat, college shirt, tie, glasses; or do anything else that helps you connect with the Customer.

Educate

This is the one that may slightly affect time of service in industries that are built around rapid pace (fast food) and may have to have an "above and beyond" action when it is warranted (e.g., a new

Customer unfamiliar with a menu). For the rest of us, it should have zero impact on productivity and be demonstrated every single time. Think of stores like Nordstrom and Apple. Their employees are brilliant about their products and applications.

=======

I love the 5 E's for the following reasons: (1) They are so simple to do, (2) they can be effective with every Customer, (3) the first four take zero time to execute, (4) they demonstrate genuine hospitality, and finally, (5) practically no one else is doing them even 25 percent of the time. The 5 E's also apply to professional service providers or internal Customer service, support, or call-center environments.

Three ways your employees engage your customers

It is important to note that not all 5 E's should be used in every customer encounter, as some might appear unrealistic in certain circumstances. There are three ways employees engage with customers: incidental contact, secondary contact, and primary contact.

Incidental contact—This is traditionally very brief, like a walk-by, seeing the Customers (coming within ten feet), but not necessarily coming in direct contact with them where you are going to have a conversation. This can be absolutely anyone in your business, from the President to the maintenance personnel. In these cases, only the first two E's should be executed every time and take a total of two seconds to execute:

1. Eye contact
2. Ear-to-ear smile

Secondary contact—This type of contact with the Customer is usually some type of support team, e.g. hostess, greeter, or receptionist.
The first three E's should be executed every time, and these also
take a total of two seconds to execute simultaneously:

1. Eye contact

2. Ear-to-ear smile

3. Enthusiastic greet

Primary contact—This encounter is more involved. It is typically
with the main person who is providing the service, e.g. a service
provider, account executive, consultant, or customer service rep.
All five E's need to be executed every time. The first three only take
a few seconds to execute, the fourth and fifth 'E's' are a little more
detailed, can be done extremely quickly and efficiently, and are
where the relationships are made, and expertise is demonstrated.

1. Eye contact

2. Ear-to-ear smile

3. Enthusiastic greet

4. Engage

   · Use your name
   · Use Customer's name
   · Provide Secret Service (FORD, customer intelligence)

5. Educate

   · Ask "Is there is anything else I can do for you?"

Prehiring screening tool
If you are looking for people who have the potential to be Customer-centric service providers, evaluating the 5 E's might be your most

powerful tool. Many of our consulting clients have incorporated the 5 E's into their interview process, literally counting the times an employee candidate demonstrates each.

5 E'S ENGAGEMENT INDICATOR

Number of times during the interview that . . .

____ eye contact was made

____ ear-to-ear smiles took place

____ enthusiasm was displayed

____ engagement with the interview occurred naturally

____ educated answers to interview questions were explored thoroughly

While I believe most employee candidates do have the potential to provide excellent Customer service, not all will. As I discussed earlier (chapter 3), the vast majority of the time you will not find people with high Service Aptitude; therefore, it is the company's responsibility to train to dramatically increase employees' Service Aptitude. Yet the real dilemma is knowing who has the potential and who doesn't. The 5 E's can tell you if candidates have the Service Aptitude potential. During the interview process, if candidates are not smiling, making eye contact, and showing enthusiasm, then pass. They do not have the potential to be even average at providing good Customer service. No amount of Customer service training will change them. The biggest key to trusting the engagement indicator is having an interviewer who also constantly displays the 5 E's.

Smile index

CEO Chip Conley, founder of Joie de Vivre Hotels, shares a great example called the Smile Index in his book, *Emotional Equations*.

> I can get a true sense of any place within seconds by observing the quantity and quality of the employees' smiles. My emotional antennae could pick up whether they were genuine or just a mask.[40]

Beat the greet

My family and I enjoyed a week's vacation at one of the resorts I worked with, the beautiful Hotel del Coronado, just outside San Diego. The Coronado is one of the finest resorts in the United States, one that prides itself on legendary Customer service. One of my takeaways was how every associate greeted us as we passed them, before we could greet them. I have always preached the "ten feet greet," where whenever you come within ten feet of a Customer, you should greet them. Never allow a Customer to greet you first. Think about it: if every one of your employees was trained to beat the Customer to the greet, it would create a pretty strong service culture. At many businesses, many employees do not even greet at all, regardless of whether they're doing it proactively or reactively. I even told my three sons that no one should ever say hello to us before we say hello to them, not only people we know, but strangers on an elevator or passing by on the street.

Sign language

Consistently acknowledging a Customer first does not happen in most businesses. Many times, employees are too focused on a task, working with an existing Customer and feeling it would be rude to interrupt the person they are working with to say hello to another Customer. In other cases, the employee may not be the one who is going to be helping the Customer; they may just be passing by. Therefore, they think greeting does not apply to them. "Beat the greet" applies to every employee in every situation. If you are tied up with another Customer or just passing through that department and will never be the one to directly interact with that Customer, use sign language: smile, nod, and acknowledge the Customer's existence as a guest on your property. This accomplishes two things. It establishes a warm and friendly atmosphere, and most importantly, it lets the Customer know that you are aware that they are there, that they exist, and that you will accommodate them as soon as you are able. Picture this: if everyone, Customers and team members, wore the exact same outfits (e.g., white shirt, black pants, no name tags), would you be able to tell who the Customers are and who the employees are by the hospitality gestures they demonstrate?

Aggressively friendly

Too many times, you watch an employee not look away from what they are doing (e.g., their computer) to make eye contact or smile until the Customer is physically within a foot of them. I love the term "aggressively friendly," which I use to refer to an employee who seeks eye contact and smiles from long distances.

Periodic acknowledgment

I was standing in line waiting to check in for my room at the Trump Towers Hotel in Chicago. About a minute into my wait, the front-desk receptionist, who was checking in the guest in front of me, said, "I will be right with you, sir." I smiled and didn't think anything of it, and shortly thereafter I was being checked in. About a minute into her checking me in, she acknowledged the person standing behind me by saying, "I will be right with you, ma'am." It was something so small, but I loved it. This simple, periodic touch told the next guest, *I am aware of you and will be right with you*, without making the guest she was working with feel as if she was rushing.

Genuine hospitality aptitude is based on our cultural differences

An interesting study of "touch behaviors" is found in the book *The Blessing* by Gary Smalley and John Trent:

> We know that for many people, meaningful touch simply wasn't a part of growing up. For me (author John Trent), growing up in Arizona, the cultural norm was, "It's okay to hug your horse, but not your kids!" Sociologist Sidney Jourand studied the touch behavior of pairs of people in coffee shops around the world. The difference between cultures was staggering. In San Juan, Puerto Rico, people touched on average 180 times per hour. In Paris, France, it was 110 times per hour. In Gainesville, FL, 2 times per hour. And in London, England, 0 times per hour.[41]

Outlove your competition

"Outlove your competition" is one of my favorite sayings. Think about it. Nearly everything can be copied: the products or services that you sell, your décor, website functionality, menu, and prices. Can you really outwork your competition? Outthink them? Maybe not, but the one way you can get a distinct competitive advantage is by outloving the businesses you compete against. The only way to do that is to stop the typical squawking that goes on about how difficult Customers can be, and just start appreciating them.

Hold internal Customer appreciation moments

I am not talking about simply having a Customer appreciation event or week, or starting a VIP program, which are all good practices to implement. What I am talking about is having internal Customer appreciation awareness campaigns. This will dramatically change the mind-set of your employees, even yourself. Far too many businesses sit around and discuss how difficult their Customers can be, how demanding they are, how they have unrealistic expectations. You hear employees and managers too often talk about that one Customer who is never happy and always wants something for free. I truly believe that this is a minute percentage of our Customer base; however, it seems like so much more because they are so frequently discussed.

Do you want to have high Service Aptitude? Do you want your employees to have compassion and empathy for your Customers? Then start having employees talk about their favorite Customers, the ones who make them love their jobs. Have your employees tell stories of the times when they have had the biggest impact on a Customer's day. Companies need to create several outlets where employees can share and hear about how lucky they are to have so many good Customers who count on them and are great to do business with. This will change the tone from "us versus them" to genuine caring about your Customers and will make everyone on your team grateful that your Customers are giving you—and not your competition—their business.

Give more than people expect, don't keep
score, and don't wait for them to do their
part. Just do what you promised and a little
more. If you borrow someone's truck or car,
give it back to them with more gas and
cleaner than how they gave it to you.

Are doctor/patient relationships overrated?

Want more evidence of how important demonstrations of caring and compassion can be in the medical world? Consider the following findings from the book *Blink*, by Malcolm Gladwell.

- The chance of a doctor being sued has hardly anything to do with the number of mistakes he or she makes.

- Research shows that highly skilled doctors get sued, in many cases a lot more than doctors who make many mistakes. In nearly every single malpractice case, the patient was quoted as saying something negative about how the doctor made them feel.

- A large number of people who did sustain an injury due to negligence never sued their doctor. Why? Because of the bond they had with the doctor. They would never consider suing the doctor or his practice, even though there was negligence on the part of their doctor.[42]

These findings reveal that patients don't file lawsuits simply because they've received poor medical care. It is how their doctor treated them on a personal level. Traditionally, people don't sue doctors they like.

3-2-1

An excellent technique for reconnecting with past clients is having your employees do the following on a weekly basis:

- Send out **3** emails to existing clients.
- Send out **2** cards to existing clients.
- Call **1** existing client on the phone.

The 3-2-1 system is best used in dealing with existing Customers with whom you are reaching out in a nonreactive way. It is a cold, out-of-the-blue act of reengaging the client, without any solicitation of product or services. For instance:

> Hello Don,
>
> Happy spring! I hope this note finds you doing well. You crossed my mind and I thought I would say hello and see how you are doing.
>
> I am not sure if I have told you how much I have enjoyed working with you. You have been an absolute pleasure to do business with, and having clients like you is the reason why I truly love what I do. I hope you and your family have an opportunity to enjoy the beautiful spring and have some fun getaways planned.
>
> Always at your service,
> Michael
> Relationship Manager

Some companies incorporating the 3-2-1 concept use a log for employees to track whom they have emailed, sent a card to, and called this week:

Send 3 emails to existing clients ~ Send out 2 cards to existing clients ~ Call 1 existing client on the phone			
Date	Emailed	Sent Card	Called

The key is to schedule executing the 3-2-1 either first thing in the morning or last thing before you shut down and go home for the day.

An interactive revolution

Initially, the Internet reduced people skills and human interaction. I do have to recognize that with the explosion of social media, there has been a dramatic increase in "human interaction" again. Now, this is completely different and will not replace the necessary "people skill" training companies have to incorporate. In *The Thank You Economy*, author Gary Vaynerchuk captures this very well.

> The cold Internet suddenly turned into an interactive revolution as people seek out what everyone is up to. Our periodic social media browse allows us to check in on everyone.

We check Facebook and comment on a friend's posting, or we click on "like" upon seeing our friend's status. We tweet a great article or how far we have come achieving our goals. Social media has allowed us to scan our network within minutes to learn what is going on, what people are thinking and doing, faster than ever before. It also has allowed us to increase our network of influence and acquaintances ten fold by re-connecting with classmates from twenty-five years ago with whom we still share the bond of youth and innocence.[43]

Virtual engagement

One big trend I see becoming a critical tool in helping Customer service reps, call centers, and anyone who has conference calls build stronger relationships is virtual calls. Picture your Customers having the ability to click a button on your website to have a Skype call with your employees. It may only be one-way communication, where the Customer can see the employee only, or two-way communication, where they can see each other. Regardless, seeing someone face to face forces employees to stay engaged, ensures they will not be distracted by anything else, and increases the amount of smiling and overall friendliness.

If your purpose is truly selflessness,
your own benefits, whether they're personal
fulfillment or financial, will be greater
than you had ever hoped.

Relationship centers

Often the contact/call center is the only interaction Customers ever have with companies, so it would make sense that organizations ensure this be an incredible experience. Unfortunately, that is typically not the case. There are several reasons; besides management not giving call centers the resources and training necessary, the Customer service representatives' responsibilities have evolved significantly. Today, they are asked to do so much more, juggling multiple channels of communications. Companies have to look at their call centers, and the role their Customer service reps have, totally differently. It is no longer a call center, rather a relationship center. In a great article titled "The Future of Contact Centers in the Age of the Customer," Nicola Millard shared a study done with contact center experts, which revealed that they expect webchat to become one of the primary ways Customers will communicate with companies. As Customers are increasingly starting their journey online or on a smartphone, webchat is an easy way of having a conversation without leaving their browser or app. Video chat is also expected to explode in the next five years.[44]

Guardians of your Customer experience

Contact centers are more critical than ever to businesses. Today, they are the ones that understand Customer demand, what Customers are contacting organizations about. Companies need to shift from the old paradigm of the call center as a "call factory" to relationship builders and "guardians of the Customer experience." What else needs to change is the traditional key performance indicators (KPIs) for contact centers, such as transactional metrics like average call handling time, which is not Customer centric. Like anything, if you don't have executive sponsorship, nothing will change.[45]

Hospitality rules at home

Giving service to someone is not something you do or deliver; it is something you are, and it is *in* you. It needs to start at home. I want my three boys, Johnni, Cal, and Bo, to have not only high Service Aptitude, but also human aptitude. Not because they will someday make a better living, but because it is who they are—an intuitive part of their being. I teach them that there is no such thing as a stranger, just a friend they haven't met yet. I want them to be natural "day makers." In order to do so, we play games and have contests all the time in public. Here are a few examples:

- **Beat the greet**—Who can smile and say hello to the most strangers while walking down the street, or in an elevator, at a mall, and at airports?

- **Show appreciation**—Thank everyone, not just the people who serve or wait on us, but policemen, TSA security, and especially men and women in military uniform. It is so cool to watch a TSA security person's face change from serious to surprise and then smile because someone actually thanked them for the job they are doing. My son Cal really does a great job to go out of his way to make sure all military personnel he comes within twenty feet of are thanked.

- **Engaging**—I have taught my sons how to find out about other people's FORD (family, occupation, recreation, and dreams). For instance, when we are at a restaurant or in a taxi, my boys try to see who can get the most personal information out of the service provider. Rarely do people ask cab drivers questions about their jobs or personal lives. They love to share, and it keeps my boys focused on other people versus talking about themselves. It also teaches them the value of showing interest in others, and how easy it is to get someone to go from transactional to enthusiastic.

Ultimate hospitality test

I recently came across a great way to test if a person has that service DNA, a test that can be used in interviews as well as just in
life by asking them if they can tell you the first name of the janitor
at their school, or landscaper, or housekeeper, or even the pizza
delivery guy. I believe this tells a lot about a person and how they
were raised. While driving my oldest son, Johnni, back to college,
I gave him some dating advice: "When you go out with a girl for
the first time, ask her if she knows the name of any of the following people she may have had in her life: landscaper, housekeeper,
handyman, janitor at school, etc. If she doesn't know, don't have a
second date."

While the ability to deliver world-class Customer service
depends on an inherent aptitude that is within us, the techniques of
how to effectively deliver that unique and special Customer experience everyone desires can indeed be taught. It's never too early in
the hiring process or the orientation process—or in life—to train
yourself, your employees, and others on the 5 E's.

10

DEPARTMENT OF CUSTOMER DEFENSE
No unhappy Customers left behind

The answer's yes.

Are you getting enough complaints?

Think about the last several times you had a disappointing experience as a Customer. Did you tell anyone at the company? You left a business frustrated or hung up the phone more stressed than before you called. If you are like most people, you don't bother to waste your time sharing your displeasure with anyone at the business that disappointed you. Why? Because most Customers don't think anyone really cares, no one really wants to hear about it, or they will think you are trying to get away with something. So why would a Customer want to waste the time? How often does this play out in your business, Customers leaving unhappy without letting anyone know?

If we are not making it easy for our Customers to give feedback, then it is happening to us more than any of us realize. Our

Customers have better things to do with their time than hunt us down and complain and then feel that it didn't make a difference.

Give permission and make it easy for them to share

There are several ways to give permission to our Customers to communicate with us. Now, I am not talking about Customer measurement devices that ask Customers their level of satisfaction and how likely they are to refer. While that is vitally important, what I am referring to is something totally different. I'm talking about giving your Customers permission to communicate easily, in a nonthreatening way, and not only giving them permission, but also asking for their advice and their feedback, both positive and negative. Few companies ask their Customers for praise, and lose the opportunity to celebrate and perpetuate outstanding performance. However, even fewer companies have the courage to ask their Customers for feedback if their experience was below what they were expecting.

It is so simple. It is just marketing to your Customer on everything: invoices, orders, emails, at checkout, on the website, even in restrooms. Here are some examples of what companies have used:

- "Please tell us about your experience. It is very important for us to know how we are doing."

- "We want your advice on how we can be better."

- "Did we hit the mark today? Tell us. Did we miss? Tell us, please!"

- "Was someone a hero for you today? We want to recognize them."

- "Were we the best part of your day? If you can't answer yes, we need to know why."

How accessible are you?

Umpqua Bank, based in Portland, Oregon, states that Customer service is what separates them from other banks. Doesn't every bank say that? The difference is Umpqua backs it up. First, Umpqua Bank's Customer service vision is "Making sure every Customer who walks into our doors is a better person for having banked with us."

Umpqua Bank is aggressive at inviting Customer feedback. If you have a question or comment and want to take it right to the top, every location has a phone in the lobby, with a sign next to it that reads, "Let's talk." Pick it up and you get CEO Ray Davis's office. You can pick up the phone and tell him what you think the bank is doing right and what you think it can do better, or you can ask him anything you'd like. There is a sign that hangs in every location: "Welcome to the World's Greatest Bank." This is not a tagline; it is a state of mind. As they like to say, "It's where an errand turns into a pleasant escape." Each Umpqua Bank offers a place where their customers can hang out, surf the Internet, or have a latte.

A complaining client is giving us the opportunity to make things right; it's the silent ones that hurt us. They don't remain silent once they leave our business.

Walking the talk

As the owner of a chain of upscale salons and spas in Northeast Ohio, I have always tried to make it easy for guests to get in touch with me. For years I have had signs posted which say: "I want to know about your experience and have provided my direct email."

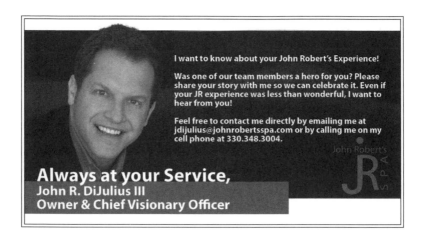

I want to know about your John Robert's Experience!

Was one of our team members a hero for you? Please share your story with me so we can celebrate it. Even if your JR experience was less than wonderful, I want to hear from you!

Feel free to contact me directly by emailing me at jdijulius@johnrobertsspa.com or by calling me on my cell phone at 330.348.3004.

Always at your Service,
John R. DiJulius III
Owner & Chief Visionary Officer

I thought this was successful because every so often I would get an email sharing feedback. However, I realized if I really wanted to back up our experience, I needed to show our guests that I was serious about hearing from them. So I added my cell phone number. This is also posted on the John Robert's website. My salons and spas see over ten thousand Customers every month.

To my surprise, I didn't get as many phone calls as I thought I would, but what I did get was a dramatic increase in guests emailing me. Even though I had always offered my email in the past, the mere fact that I was willing to share my cell phone number made them realize that I really wanted to know, which made them care more about my business and want to help me by sharing when things are not as good as they could be. The other surprising thing was the increase in positive stories I started receiving. This allowed me to recognize, share, and celebrate these stories company-wide, which in turn perpetuated that type of behavior.

The two most important words when serving others

I think the two most powerful words employees need to have permeated throughout their consciousness are "compassion" and "empathy." When you genuinely serve with compassion and empathy, your Customer service is on a completely different level. The question is, how do you teach compassion and empathy? How do you make them more than just buzzwords and platitudes? The top world-class Customer experience organizations constantly put their employees in the shoes of the Customer. When your employees really understand the plight of the Customer—what the Customer is going through, their daily battles (see chapter 5)—it starts to crystallize how critically important the experience your employees deliver is, as well as how genuine the caring they show each Customer is.

Customers are not rational

Emotions outpower and manipulate our reasoning, and emotion leads to action. Customer experience can trigger a wide array of emotions that can have a great influence on repeat business. Sometimes we don't know why we like going to a certain place, but something drives us to stop there. We make logical reasons of why, defending the fact that it is based on convenience or something else; but the truth is, the business that delivered a unique experience has emotional capital that can be subconscious. On the other hand, when we hear of a brand and have negative thoughts, most often the case is that one time a poor experience left a permanent negative stamp in our mind.

Understand that it is rational to be irrational

One of the most confusing and frustrating things to employees is the unreasonable way Customers can react to something that seems so minor. However, when a Customer has expectations—not unrealistic expectations, but simple ones about what it will be like to do business with you—and the business fails to deliver, the Customer can get emotional. For instance, the Customer could be having a stressful day, counting on the one company they can always trust (these are typically our best Customers), yet this one time, they not only didn't get to escape, but their stress level increased as well. Even though it may have been the first time the company has messed up with this Customer, the Customer can react emotionally. It is critical that Customer emotions be part of employee service-recovery training—especially for dissatisfied Customers. Once employees understand there is a good probability of a Customer reacting emotionally instead of rationally, they won't take it personally and are better able to make a brilliant comeback.

Everything is our problem

Write it down. "*Everything* is our problem." Say it out loud. Too many businesses take the "It's not our fault" approach when something goes wrong that a Customer doesn't like. This mentality leads the business to punish the Customer, which means you won the argument but lost the Customer.

At John Robert's Spa, we had a situation that demonstrated this very well. Guests would sometimes leave their valuables (jewelry or cell phone) in the pockets of the spa robes. This meant the guests' possessions could get washed and/or lost when we did our laundry. Now, the first thing one of my managers did to make sure we were not liable was post a sign in each locker in the changing room that read, "We are not responsible for any valuables left behind." A huge negative cue (chapter 4)! I was not happy when I found out about this. The bottom line is, if a guest comes to me and complains we washed her iPhone, sign or no sign, we are replacing it.

I immediately had the sign changed from a threatening message to a courtesy message: "Please remember to check your robe and locker for all your valuables." While that was better, it didn't eliminate the problem. On occasions, guests were still leaving their valuables in our robes. We had to figure out how we could fix this. One option was to train our spa attendants to do a better job checking every robe every time before washing. However, they are human; some will slip by. Because we always feel that everything is our problem to solve, no matter whose fault, we were forced to figure out a solution. We did: we found a supplier who provides pocketless robes. Problem solved.

Find your pocketless robes

If you really train everyone in your company to have the mind-set that *everything* is your problem, and you remove the victim mentality of "It is our Customer's fault," your company's Customer experience will elevate to new heights. You'll find solutions that eliminate the problems and make your company more efficient—and your Customers happier.

Not the hospital's fault

One of the hospitals we consult with, due to its significant size, has always battled with a large percentage of its patients being late for appointments. This is a huge problem. It wasn't a result of patients not respecting the hospital's time, or their poor planning. It was because the hospital is so large (literally stretching for several blocks). Once patients found the correct building and parking garage, then the real challenge began: walking and finding the office in a maze of buildings and hallways. Obviously this is a logistical nightmare for a business that works off tight scheduling.

Solution #1: Threaten and punish

The hospital could warn the patients that they will forfeit their appointment if they are late but will still be charged for the visit. Obviously this is not exactly the approach a business wants to take with its Customers.

Solution #2: Allow for this in hospital's scheduling

Another option is the hospital could allow more time built in with each patient to account for tardiness. This results in fewer appointments per day. Not good financially for the hospital, and not good for the patients, because that would mean less availability and would necessitate a longer wait to get in to see their doctor.

Solution #3: Own the problem

Realizing how critical this is to running a successful business, the hospital finally did two things: (1) it staffed more recognizable volunteers all over the hospital to help direct patients to their destination, and (2) it created a GPS app for smartphones, which shows patients, once they park, how to get to the proper place on the property (e.g., building P, office 515).

Customers expect companies to share their burdens

World-class Customer service companies have long since realized that what was once a Customer responsibility is no longer. This is why your bank tells you when your mortgage payment is due and your pharmacy reminds you that it's time to refill your prescription. Amazon even notifies you when you already purchased a particular title for your Kindle two years ago, and refuses to let you accidentally pay for it again. These are all examples of owning a problem and dramatically improving the Customer's experience.[46]

Customer aggravation index

Some companies have figured out a way to track Customer aggravation. One example is how FedEx has pioneered the development of a metric that tracks how many Customers it angers on a daily basis and how mad it makes them. By holding focus groups with Customers, FedEx gathered a long list of things it had done to aggravate Customers over the years. Once FedEx narrowed down this list to a reasonable number of problems, it had Customers rank the order from 1 to 10 with 10 being the most egregious. So a 10 would be when FedEx loses a package and never recovers it. A minor aggravation rating of a 1 or 2 might be a package that is an hour or two late. Every day, FedEx tracks occurrences of these problems, multiplies the frequency by the severity, and rolls it up into an index that measures Customer aggravation levels. It turns out that this index is directly correlated to disloyalty. Many other companies have now created their own customer-aggravation index and track it daily.[47]

Total transparency

cj Advertising, headquartered in Nashville, Tennessee, is an advertising firm exclusively serving personal-injury attorneys. Arnie Malham, president of cj Advertising, has a fresh and totally unique perspective on the way he runs his business. For example, Arnie allows all his Customers to publicly post their satisfaction scores and share feedback. All his Customers can see how the company is doing with regard to overall satisfaction. He does the same thing for his employees. Each quarter they are asked to fill out a survey stating their level of satisfaction (1–5) and to share any and all comments they have. All of his Customers can see this. They can see what his other Customers are saying, and how cj Advertising is being rated. I have never heard of such transparency! I asked Arnie about this and he said, "Most people say I need to have my head examined for doing this. However, we like the pressure of knowing that if we don't take care of our Customers, or don't react when something goes wrong, it will be made public."

I have read the comments and have interviewed several of cj's clients, and they say this is one of the reasons they love to do business with cj Advertising. cj is a forward-moving, robust company largely as a result of Arnie's appetite for critical feedback. While most companies adopt the "head in the sand" approach with regard to criticism, Arnie actually goes looking for it. By asking his clients what cj can do better, he puts cj in a better position to actually get better!

Anti-no zone

My employees don't need to ask permission to do anything for a Customer except use the word no. And to my knowledge, we have never given permission. It doesn't mean everything is a yes, but no is the word heard most often in business. Train your employees to eliminate it, treat it like a swear word, and focus on alternatives. An article titled "Stop Trying to Delight Your Customers," which appeared in the *Harvard Business Review*, demonstrates the power of removing the word no from your company's vocabulary. Ameriprise Financial asked its Customer service reps to capture every instance in which they were forced to tell a Customer no. While auditing the no's, the company found many dated policies that had been outmoded by regulatory changes, or systems, or process improvements. During its first year of "capturing the no's," Ameriprise modified or eliminated twenty-six policies. It has since expanded the program by asking frontline reps to come up with other process efficiencies, generating $1.2 million in savings as a result.[48]

The "AskOnce" promise
Another great example from the *HBR* article explains how some companies are making low effort by the Customer the cornerstone of their service value proposition. South Africa's Nedbank instituted an "AskOnce" promise, which guarantees that the rep who picks up the phone will own the Customer's issue from start to finish. The immediate mission is clear: leadership must train frontline employees on mitigating disloyalty by reducing the effort Customers must make. Most Customers encounter loyalty-eroding problems when they engage with Customer service:

- 56 percent report having to re-explain an issue.

- 57 percent report having to switch from the web to the phone to solve a problem.

- 59 percent report expending moderate to high effort to resolve an issue.

- 59 percent report being transferred.

- 62 percent report having to repeatedly contact the company to resolve an issue.[49]

The answer's yes . . . Now what's the question?
This is one of my favorite Customer service mantras. When a Customer approaches any of my employees, before they even say anything to my employees, I want my employee to say yes. Just say yes

before a Customer can ask you something. The Customer will be shocked and your employee will figure out a way to do it. Customers are not going to ask you for something unreasonable. Here is Seth Godin's thoughts on saying yes:

> Yes is an opportunity and yes is an obligation. The closer we get to people who are confronting the resistance on their way to making a ruckus, the more they let us in, the greater our obligation is to focus on the yes. There will always be a surplus of people eager to criticize, nitpick, or recommend caution. Your job, at least right now, is to reinforce the power of the yes.[50]

11

REVOLUTIONIZING YOUR INDUSTRY
Creating an experience epiphany

Let's go make some history today, do things that people will talk about for decades to come, which may end up in the history books, redefining the way it is currently being done.

Experience epiphany

An "experience epiphany" fills a gap Customers didn't know was there. What was once considered impossible is now the standard experience everyone else is trying to duplicate. Experience epiphanies rarely occur in familiar surroundings. Steve Jobs said it best: "The key to thinking differently is to perceive things differently, through the lenses of a trailblazer. And to see things through these lenses, you must force your brain to make connections it otherwise would have missed."

My favorite Customer service models are the ones that are so unique to their industry. Too many businesses operate like blind sheep and do what has always been done. Then you have companies like Amazon, Apple, Starbucks, Nordstrom, and Zappos, which introduce such simple concepts, unheard of in their industries, and dominate even in tough economic times. Listening to your Customers is acceptable for driving incremental Customer satisfaction, but it hardly generates breakthroughs. A better description for what great companies deliver is called an "experience epiphany." That's a vision of what the Customer will want in the future and won't be able to live without.

Leaders are fascinated by the future, restless for change, impatient for progress, and deeply dissatisfied with the status quo. They are never satisfied with the present, because in their head they can see a better future, and the friction between what is and what could be burns them, propels them forward.

—Steve Jobs

Filling a gap Customers didn't know was there

Steve Jobs, Howard Schultz, Jeff Bezos, and Tony Hsieh did not think conventionally when they built their business model. Nor did they underestimate the power of an emotional experience that doesn't always fit conveniently onto a spreadsheet or isn't initially understood by Wall Street. Each launched a revolution in their respective industries precisely because they had a bigger vision than their competitors.

In the book *The Innovation Secrets of Steve Jobs*, author Carmine Gallo shares how Apple has become the world's best retailer by thinking differently than most other retailers. There are no cashiers at the Apple Store; there are specialists—even "geniuses"—but no cashiers. There are no salespeople; there are consultants, concierges, experts, and personal shoppers—but no salespeople. Although the Apple Stores have no commissioned sales staff, they generate more revenue per square foot than most other widely recognized brands. Apple's famous glass-cube store on New York's Fifth Avenue reportedly generates higher sales per square foot than its neighbors, Saks and Tiffany's—significantly higher. Apple's revenue has been pegged at $4,032 per square foot per year. Compare that with Tiffany's at $2,600 or Best Buy at $930. After studying Customer service leaders, Apple arrived at several criteria that would help the Apple Stores stand apart:

- Design uncluttered stores.

- Allow Customers to test-drive products.

- Offer a concierge experience.

- Make it easy to buy.

- Offer one-to-one training.

Transformational breakthroughs are rarely the result of focus groups. Customers didn't ask for the iTunes store, but today they can't live without it. Customers didn't ask for the iPhone, but today millions of people can't live without it. Apple has innovated around the retail experience by changing people's expectations of what a retail experience could be.[51]

The Zappos buzz

Why all the fuss over Zappos? By now, you have probably heard countless legendary stories about a company started out of a living room. Zappos' goal was to get people to buy shoes online, and it succeeded. About ten years after it was started, Zappos was sold for more than $1 billion. All this was done during one of the worst economic recessions in our lifetime. Zappos' business was built using world-class Customer service—not just relative to other e-commerce retailers, but world-class Customer service by anyone's standards.

Consider this: Zappos sells shoes online, a concept no one ever thought would take off due to the unpredictable and inconsistent sizes of different brands and styles. But it does sell a lot of shoes online—more than $1 billion dollars' worth. It has a cult-like employee base of over 1,300 associates referred to as Zapponians, yet the company pays salaries that are often below market rate. The average hourly worker makes a modest wage per year. All employees receive four weeks of training. Midway through their training, all trainees are offered a $3,000 quitting bonus. "Zappos is built around one single concept: Deliver 'WOW' through service and everyone is brainwashed to execute that. The key drivers of our growth at Zappos has been repeat Customers and word of mouth. Our philosophy has been to take most of the money we would have spent on paid advertising and invest it in Customer service and the Customer experience instead, letting our Customers do the marketing for us through word of mouth," says Tony Hsieh, Zappos founder and president.[52]

A Zappos Customer enjoys free shipping, free returns, and a retailer that always under promises and over delivers. Zappos promises you will receive your order in two to three days and sometimes sends your shipment next-day air. It also has toll-free Customer support answered by a human being 24/7, a personal buying service, and free socks. What made Zappos act like a hospitality company that just happened to sell shoes online? Survival! Early on, the company could not afford to spend money on marketing, so the sales strategy was quite simple: *Make Customers so happy and pleasantly surprised that they buy again and tell their friends.* As a result of its success, these staple amenities that exceeded traditional service experiences elsewhere are still part of the Zappos experience today.

However, just empowering your frontline employees doesn't mean they will actually do it or know how to be effective. That is where Zappos doesn't hope that most employees get it; it makes sure of it. It's a hard job, answering phones and talking to Customers for hours at a time. So when Zappos hires new employees, it provides a four-week training period that immerses them in the company's strategy, culture, and obsession with Customers. People get paid their full salary during this period. Another example of how effectively Zappos uses its phones as a branding device is what happens when a Customer calls looking for a particular style of shoe, in a specific size, and for which Zappos may be out of stock. In those instances, every rep is trained to research at least three competitors' websites, and if the shoes are found in stock, to direct the Customer to the competitor.[53]

Measuring the wrong metrics can damage your Customer's experience

The two most popular performance metrics by which call centers and Customer service reps are tracked are average call time and time-to-resolution. These are dinosaur drivers that management needs to move away from. They are anti–service friendly. They make your reps solely task focused and dehumanize their roles, which dramatically reduces their work satisfaction and increases turnover. Zappos looks at its call center as an investment in marketing, a strategy to create loyalty through "wow" moments and emotional connections. Zappos still uses metrics, but only to support the Customer experience, which has proven to be quite successful financially as well. The article "A Zappos Lesson in Customer Service Metrics" from Customer Service Investigator shares Zappos' best practices, such as how it feels it is "more important that we make an emotional connection with the Customer, rather than just quickly getting them off the phone," says Derek Carder, Customer loyalty operations manager for Zappos. That is why Zappos places more value on the percent of time an agent spends on the phone than on quick time-to-resolution or processing high call volumes. This metric—personal service level—is a way to "empower the team to utilize their time how they see it best promotes Customer loyalty," Carder says. Quality instead of quantity.[54]

Rewarding the right behavior produces the right results. Customer service reps are not machines; they are people who enjoy building relationships. Also noted is how CSRs at Zappos are expected to spend at least 80 percent of their time in Customer-facing interactions. It doesn't matter if that's one call or a hundred. Reps who achieve this target get to spin "the wheel of happiness" to win gift cards and other rewards. Those who fall below the 80 percent line receive coaching.[55] Zappos uses little advertising or traditional marketing; its marketing is word of mouth and Customer loyalty. It does this by measuring four factors on a hundred-point scale called the "Happiness Experience Form":

1. Did the agent try twice to make a personal emotional connection (PEC)?
2. Did they keep the rapport going after the Customer responded to their attempt?
3. Did they address unstated needs?
4. Did they provide a "wow experience"?

A rep who averages fewer than fifty points per month on the Happiness Experience Form will receive extra training, while top performers are rewarded with paid hours off and other incentives.[56]

World-class e-commerce

Too often, the only companies that concern themselves with excellent online Customer service standards are companies where e-commerce is their primary business. However, every company today has an online presence. Your website is one of your biggest marketing and branding tools even if it accounts for a minor percentage of your sales. World-class service cannot stop at the brick and mortar. One of my biggest complaints about most websites is trying to find a company's phone number. Typically it is buried somewhere on the contact page. When you visit Zappos.com, it is impossible to visit any page and not see its phone number predominantly displayed.

"To be the earth's most Customer-centric company"

"To be the earth's most Customer-centric company" is a pretty ambitious goal, but I wouldn't bet against the author of that statement, Jeff Bezos. *Success* magazine featured the founder and president of Amazon in its August 2011 issue, and, as always, the pioneer stressed how Amazon's success is built around fanatical drive on the Customer experience. Some excerpts from Bezos: "The customer experience is the critical guiding hand. Our vision is to be the earth's most customer-centric company; to build a place where people can come to find and discover anything they might want to buy online." With that type of vision from the president, is it any wonder why Amazon has revolutionized not only e-commerce, but also retailing and publishing? The article reads, "If the Internet were rock and roll, Bezos was its Elvis." Bezos cites the fundamental differences between an entrepreneur and professional management: "Entrepreneurs are more stubborn about the vision and keep working on the details. One of the dangers about bringing in professional managers is the first thing they want to alter is the vision. The rule of thumb is to be stubborn on the big things and flexible on the details."[57]

May we call you?

I had a surprising experience one time after I made a purchase on Amazon: I realized that I had selected the wrong product. I cringed and immediately started thinking about how difficult this was going to be to fix over the Internet. I was convinced it was going to take at least thirty minutes to resolve. I immediately found a "Customer Service" link, which brought me to "How would you like to contact us?" with three options: email, phone, or chat. I clicked on "phone." This brought up "Have us call you right now," with an area for me to enter my phone number and the choice to "Call me now" or "Call me in five minutes." I typed in my phone number and selected "Call me now" and within seconds my phone was ringing. My issue was resolved in a few short minutes. What a wonderful experience and surprise!

Amazon revolutionized everything. It didn't just start off being a site that sells; it became an early social network site for book fans. It allowed its Customers to review the products they were buying. This feedback from Customers was originally controversial. They were allowed to write bad reviews of books, and competitors couldn't understand why a bookseller would allow such a thing. Who would buy a book that someone panned? Some local bookstores have employees write reviews of books they like, but they just ignore books they don't like. It was all part of Bezos's plan to create the world's most Customer-centric company. Within a few weeks after starting the Customer review process, he said, "I started receiving letters from well-meaning folks saying that perhaps you don't understand your business. You make money when you sell things. Why are you allowing negative reviews on your Web site? But our point of view is we will sell more if we help people make purchasing decisions." These tactics worked partly because they were such unusual moves. Customer reviews taught people that Amazon was a different kind of store, one that could be relied upon to point out books that were probably a waste of time and money. It helped build goodwill. It reinforced Bezos's image as an executive who actually cares about his Customers.[58]

Amex improves cardholder's experience and shareholder value

Jim Bush, EVP of world service of American Express, revolutionized the call-center experience by decreasing the stereotypical emphasis on monitoring call times and scripts for call reps and increasing relationship-building skills and techniques. Here's what he said in an interview with CNNMoney:

> We moved from being transaction-oriented—the investment and training had been all around how to complete the transaction—to building on the relationship with the customer . . . We've been able to show that increased satisfaction drives increased engagement with American Express products, and that drives shareholder value. Great service is great business. We track it all the way to shareholder value. For a promoter who is positive on American Express, we see a 10% to 15% increase in spending and four to five times increased retention, both of which drive shareholder value. In fact our operating expenses associated with service have gone down because we're more streamlined, and we limit friction points and errors . . . The training has changed. In the past, 75% of it was on how, technically, you complete the transaction. Now it's on how you create the relationship and build it through humanity, conversation, and engagement.[59]

In the book *An Amazement Revolution*, author Shep Hyken shares how American Express decided to take a different approach: de-emphasizing the metrics, training its people in unscripted "soft skills" such as listening and relationship building, and investing in new technologies that enabled them to make better Customer-specific product and service recommendations during the calls. Instead of simply trying to shorten call times, the company made the strategic decision to use the calls to improve the quality of person-to-person connection with card members. To do this, the company hired, trained, and motivated its Customer care professionals to be better, more autonomous improvisers, a major change in workplace culture that gave the frontline people much more control over the direction of the call. Since these and other changes were made, American Express has seen a rise in card member awareness of its varied products and services offerings. That improvement has been accompanied by a strong upward trend in Customers' overall satisfaction with the company. At the same time, the company's call-center retention rates have improved.[60]

Emotional connection is our true value proposition

In his book *Onward*, Howard Schultz shares insight on how Starbucks was forced to reinvent itself. Admittedly, it became overzealous for same-store sales, which eventually led to the watering down of the Starbuck's experience and to what some called the commoditization of its brand. Schultz, the company's CEO, stresses that one of the keys to the famous "transformational agenda" was the Customer experience in order to win back lost Customers:

> People come to Starbucks for coffee and human connection. We would put our customers back in the center of the experience by addressing their needs and developing programs

that recognize and reward our most loyal customers. In our stores, we would achieve operational excellence, finding new ways to deliver world-class customer service . . . When we are fully engaged, we connect with, laugh with, and uplift the lives of our customers—even if just for a few moments. Sure it starts with the promise of a perfectly made beverage, but our work goes far beyond that. It's really about human connection. Starbucks coffee is exceptional, yes, but emotional connection is our true value proposition.[61]

Super service sandwich shop

The *New York Times* article "Would You Like a Smile with That?" showed how a fast-growing British-based sandwich chain, Pret A Manger (PAM), is now invading the US market due to the significance the brand places on Customer service. PAM's service model seems impressive. Executives say that in order to encourage teamwork, the answer is to hire, pay, and promote based on qualities directly related to Customer service, like cheerfulness.

Survivor

New hires are sent to a Pret A Manger shop for a six-hour day, and then the employees there vote whether to keep them or not. 90 percent of prospects get a thumbs-up. Those who don't make the cut are sent away. The crucial factor is gaining support from existing employees. Those workers have skin in the game: bonuses are awarded based on the performance of an entire team, not individuals. Pret workers know that a bad hire could cost them money. Pret has an employee Service Aptitude test. By their third month, employees have to pass a written quiz with questions like "What is the maximum time a Customer should wait in line?" and show that they are proficient in dozens of practical criteria. Then they become "team member stars," and can move up to food-preparation positions like "hot chef," who oversees soups, pastries, and other hot foods, en route to more senior management positions.[62]

Pret also sends "mystery shoppers"—people who anonymously visit and grade the stores—to every shop each week. Those shoppers give employee-specific critiques ("Bill didn't smile," for instance). If a mystery shopper scores a shop as "outstanding," all of the employees get a per-hour bonus, based on a week's pay. "There's a lot of peer pressure," said Andrea Wareham, the human resources director at Pret. Pret reinforces the teamwork concept in other ways. When employees are promoted or pass training milestones, they receive a bonus, a payment that Pret calls a "shooting star." But instead of keeping the bonus, the employees must give the money to colleagues, people who have helped them along the way.[63]

Rewards drive Service Aptitude

Every quarter, the top 10 percent of stores (as ranked by mystery-shopper scores), receive money per employee for a party. The top executives at Pret get sixty "Wow" cards, with scratch-off rewards such as a cash prize or an iPod, to hand out each year, as well. "Rewards, through bonuses or 'outstanding' cards, affect behavior," Ms. Wareham says. Pret also has highly detailed training programs and training materials. "If people know what they are there to do, and how to do it, there's no confusion," Ms. Wareham says. Every new employee gets a thick binder of instructions. It states, for example, that employees should be "bustling around and being active" on the floor, not "standing around looking bored." It encourages them to occasionally hand out free coffee or cakes to regulars, and not "hide your true character" with Customers.[64]

Experience first, then the product

Stanley Hainsworth has been a catalyst for two of the greatest brands of modern times: Nike, as the creative director, and Starbucks, as the VP of global creativity. Hainsworth describes how great brands emotionally connect with consumers. First, he says, the best brands are those that create something that consumers didn't even know they needed. His experience working with Nike and Starbucks taught him this lesson:

> What I observed working with both companies is the rigor and unfailing attention to the product and unbelievable energy spent on creating the brand experience. I describe it as experience first and product second, because no one is going to pick up your product and try it if they don't want to buy into the experience. This experience comes through advertising, the retail environment, and the online experience—every single brand touch-point. There is a very intentional effort to inspire people to get caught up in that experience and say, "I want to try that."[65]

Making fees irrelevant

Vernon Hill was the Steve Jobs of the banking industry. Hill was the founder of Commerce Bank decades ago. He had a vision to build a bank not like any other financial institution, but rather like the most successful retailer. In the book *Uncommon Service*, written by Frances Frei and Anne Morriss, it depicts how Commerce Bank went about revolutionizing the banking industry and making fees irrelevant. The bank's niche? Convenience! Commerce targeted Customers who were fed up with the traditional bank's lack of convenience in the 1990s. The bank chose to be open seven days a week, Monday through Friday, 7:30 a.m. to 8:00 p.m. On Friday evenings (payday), drive-through windows stayed open until midnight. The bank was also open all day Saturday and Sunday. This earned Commerce the tagline of "America's most convenient bank." How did Commerce afford the cost of being the most convenient? The bank paid the lowest rates on deposits, and its Customers didn't seem to mind.[66]

Attitude versus aptitude

Commerce Bank also wanted to be world-class in Customer engagement. However, the bank found out that hiring employees who have both high technical aptitude and an outstanding attitude was not cost effective. So the bank chose attitude. Commerce set out to have the most cheerful, engaging frontline employees. They focused almost exclusively on hiring based on enthusiasm and interpersonal skills. These friendly recruits quickly blew the doors off the industry's poor reputation for service. Not only were employees nice, but they were happy and empathetic as well! They greeted Customers at the door with newspapers and walked them to their cars in bad weather. Since it hired attitude over aptitude, Commerce decided to keep things really simple. The bank's service offerings were the least in the entire banking industry. But the Customers got what they wanted—the friendliest interactions—and they didn't mind paying a premium for it (or receiving a lower rate). Commerce did things radically different from other banks: it offered the worst rates in the industry, provided little diversification in services, and made very few acquisitions, which was the conventional model for growth in the banking industry. Commerce Bank operated its banks like a hospitality company, with friendly, engaging employees. The results? The bank enjoyed a 2,000 percent stock price increase during the 1990s![67]

The best way to predict the future is to invent it

In 2013, John Robert's Spa opened a new location on the west side of Cleveland. What is unique about this location is that the first time you enter, you may question if you actually walked into a salon. There is no front desk, no computer, no printer, no receptionist sitting at a chair, not even a hostess stand. You walk into an experience area where you can test and try on the beauty products displayed on tables. On another table is a touch-screen monitor where you can look for the latest fashion style. There is a concierge that comes to you with an iPad, greets you where you are, and checks you in. The concierge is also able to visit guests while they are getting a hair service or manicure or pedicure, get them their products, check them out, and schedule their next appointment, saving the guest a few minutes after their services are done. While the guests seem to enjoy this unique experience and these conveniences, this particular location sells the highest retailing per client, three dollars more per client than any of the other John Robert's Spa locations.

Uncommon lawyers

Carter Mario Law Firm, specializing in personal injury, has six locations throughout Connecticut. Carter Mario, CEO and president, a person who is passionate about service, chose to make the client experience the law firm's strongest competitive advantage. For instance, the firm guarantees to return a client's call the same day or lunch is on Carter Mario himself. Carter Mario instituted a procedure for capturing information about each client in a format that allows everyone access. The firm was able to customize its customer management software, which is made for attorneys, by adding a "Secret Service" tab. This tab contains vital Customer intelligence, such as preferred refreshment, client's eye color, birth date, spouse and other family members' names, children's ages, hobbies, past vacations, even pets' names.[68]

Carter Mario has a short list of "non-negotiable" standards. Here are some examples:

- They are available 24/7, live, never an answering machine.

- All clients get a call back the same day, or lunch is on Carter.

- At 8:45 a.m. every day, they conduct a "morning huddle" to communicate with the staff about the priorities of the day as well to share "Customer intelligence" on any clients who are visiting the office that day.

- Front desk is never left unattended.

- Any staff member to come within five feet of a client is to smile, look the client in the eye, and say hello.

- Clients are offered Carter Mario umbrellas during poor weather.

The better the experience, the less the advertising

Research has shown that world-class Customer service organizations spend less on advertising than the rest of their industry. Why? Because they have an unpaid sales force—their existing Customers. When Carter Mario started tracking the source of incoming calls (the backbone of their business) in 2006, roughly 30 percent of their calls came from word-of-mouth/referral sources and approximately 70 percent came from paid advertising. The following figure demonstrates the positive growth of the law firm's word-of-mouth calls (2006–2012); in the last year of this period word-of-mouth/referral calls eclipsed 60 percent of total calls!

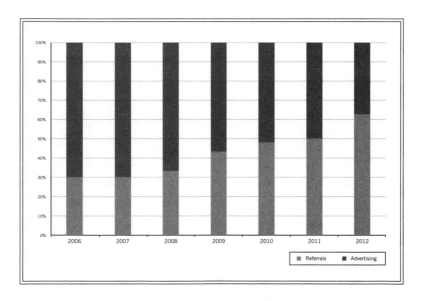

A world-class hospitality law firm

What changed or what was the driving force behind this movement? "While we thought we were client centric, we realized we were relative to injury attorneys, which means we were the best of a lousy group," says Carter Mario. "In 2007, our entire organization, including receptionists, in-take specialists, administrative positions, and attorneys, became obsessed with being a world-class Customer service company, benchmarked against anyone in any other industry." That they did! Carter Mario Law Firms are well known for their Customer service.

QuikTrip

QuikTrip is a privately held company headquartered in Tulsa, Oklahoma. QuikTrip has revolutionized the convenience store industry. QuikTrip ignored conventional wisdom, broke the model, and revolutionized an entire industry. Typically, the dynamics of the convenience store industry are 24/7 operation, low frontline wages, and an average turnover rate of 300 percent.[69]

QuikTrip's mission: "To provide opportunity for employees to grow and succeed." Those are not just words on a plaque; they are truly committed to their employees. They hire employees on the basis of their people skills, and put them first. They pay them generously and promote from within. They believe employee compensation is more important than profits and the bottom line. Full-time hires get regular medical insurance as well as a reimbursement plan from day one. Their time-off policy is unheard of for frontline employees. Not only do employees get ten to twenty-five vacation days a year (depending on tenure) plus ten days of sick pay, they can buy two extra weeks off, and request an additional ten days without pay, no questions asked. Rather than calling in sick on the morning of an absence, an employee can just request in advance a day off, giving management a heads-up opportunity to restaff without a disruption of service. As a result, QuikTrip has created an "employer market" resulting in over a thousand job applications a week. QuikTrip has grown into a company worth over $10 billion, with 13,000 employees and over 650 stores in eleven states. Those revenues place QuikTrip high on the *Forbes* listing of largest privately held companies. *Fortune* magazine has ranked QuikTrip high on the list of "Best Companies to Work For" each of the last ten years.[70]

No to luggage

Apthorp, a dry-cleaning company in the New York area, has created additional revenue streams to complement its staple dry-cleaning services. If you are a busy business traveler, routinely getting on a plane every week, you are aware of two major frustrations: (1) constantly packing and unpacking and (2) hoping that your luggage will arrive to your destination so you will have something to wear. Apthorp Cleaners has created the perfect solution: "Just say *no* to luggage and say *yes* to Clean & Pack." Clean & Pack allows Apthorp Customers to drop off their suitcase filled with dirty clothes, and Apthorp will dry-clean and repack your suitcase for you so it is ready for your next trip. Even better, they will ship the suitcase to your next destination for you.

The party bus

One of my family's annual summer vacations is to Nemacolin Woodlands Resort in Farmington, Pennsylvania. We usually go with several other families. On a particular trip, one moment that really stood out was when a group of about a dozen of us were waiting for a shuttle bus to take us from dinner back to our hotel at around 11:00 p.m. Nemacolin is such a large property that it runs shuttle buses all day and night to transport its guests from one part of the property to the next. A shuttle pulled up and as I started to enter it, the rest of my group said, "That's not Helen! We called for

Helen. We will wait." I looked at them and said, "Are you crazy? It's late, let's get on the shuttle." The kids were exhausted and I just wanted to get back to my hotel room at this point. However, the rest of my group wouldn't budge. They were dead set on waiting for Helen. So, out of curiosity, I waited to see what all the fuss was. Soon after, a shuttle pulled up, the doors swung open, and the party started.

Helen owns every moment

Helen Humphrey has been a Nemacolin legend for over nine years. Guests love her and request her shuttles all the time because she plays music and flashes the interior lights to the beat of the music (which is why she is also known as Disco Helen). She interacts with guests via the intercom, asking which passengers have never been here ("Who is a Nemacolin Virgin?") and finding all sorts of ways to entertain her passengers. She has the "Party Bus." Helen has been known to go shopping for guests and bring them items so they never have to leave the property. She also received the "Fan Mail Award" in 2011. This is given to the associate who receives the most positive name mentions. If a shuttle bus driver can find a way to provide such a uniquely memorable experience, how can each of us do the same when we interact with our Customers?

In default

The payday loan industry has one of the worst ethical business reputations going. The industry has been heavily criticized for lending irresponsibly, applying outlandish interest rates, charging excessive fees, collecting debt aggressively, and even committing fraud on occasion. The government has stepped in and implemented many radical regulations, and as a result, payday loan banks cannot even operate anymore in a growing number of US states.

Enter Advance Financial, a chain of more than fifty payday loan centers headquartered in Nashville, Tennessee. For the past two years, Advance Financial has been reinventing itself with an aggressive strategic plan to build a world-class Customer experience business. Advance Financial's sales growth in the last five years has been amazing. In the last three years alone, its sales increase was 250 percent, while the rest of the payday loan industry is notorious for being horrible at Customer service. When Advance Financial reached out to The DiJulius Group in 2012 about hiring us as its Customer service consulting firm, I asked CEO Tina Hodges the following questions: "Your company is rocking and rolling, sales are up, profit is great, no one else in your industry is delivering good Customer service; so why the need to change and tamper with success? It will be a lot of work, it is a long-term commitment, and why do you need to become the first world-class Customer service payday loan bank?" Here is how Tina answered my questions.

> We would be bringing a world-class service experience to a new segment of the population in middle Tennessee. No one treats our Customers like VIPs because in most retailers' eyes, they are not VIPs. We can change the stigma of our industry and also change the idea that this group of people deserves VIP services and that there is a place in middle Tennessee that is giving it to them. It will force others to raise the bar. The financial success it will bring our company will just be a by-product of the increased Customer satisfaction and increased employee engagement.

Advance Financial has done so much to ensure that the Customer experience is its distinct competitive advantage:

- It named a CXO (Chief Xperience Officer) and a customer and employee affairs director.

- It created a day-in-the-life video of an Advance Financial Customer that all new employees must watch in their orientation.

- It created a Customer service vision statement with pillars and a "never and always" list and rolled these out to the entire company.

- It created an online training certification of games like *Jeopardy!*, Memory, and *Wheel of Fortune*, ensuring its employees retain their Customer service training, while making it extremely entertaining.

- It created a new Customer experience at every encounter.

- It has Secret Service agent teams, made up of frontline employees throughout all their locations, to support this project and audit the experience.

How can you create an experience epiphany and revolutionize your industry?

An experience epiphany fills a gap Customers didn't know existed. What was once considered impossible is now the standard experience everyone else is trying to duplicate. It's a vision of what the Customer will want in the future and eventually won't be able to live without.

LIVING AN EXTRAORDINARY LIFE
So countless others do as well

Who are you not to be great? Who are you to be ordinary? Who are you to deny greatness? If you would deny it to yourself, you would deny it to the entire world. How dare you to be ordinary?

—GREATNESS AWAITS PS4 COMMERCIAL

I gave my best

This may sound mean or unsympathetic, but one of my least favorite sayings is "I gave my best." To me, it is an unacceptable crutch; I don't want to hear it.

My personal feeling is this: when the goal is to accomplish greatness, go where no one or team has gone before. I wasn't asking for your best effort; your best is what you *were* capable of in the past. I was expecting you to figure it out, to try a thousand ways, if need be try another thousand ways, expecting you to innovate, lose sleep, get around it, find loopholes, research, sweat like you never have before. Every extraordinary accomplishment, invention, or revolution was not a result of someone giving his or her best. Somehow that person or group found a way to do what no one else could do; they did the impossible; they did what no one had ever done before. The real issue is: it's not the effort that is in question at the moment or during the event; it's what you put into it leading up to it. Whether you win or lose, get the sale, or ace the test, it is all determined by the effort given in preparing for the event. Every match is determined long before the contest happens. So the next time you fail, before you want to make yourself feel better by saying "I did my best," consider if you had given your best in the preparation. The actual effort given in the event has the littlest to do with the outcome.

Each of us has the ability to impact thousands of people's lives through providing genuine care for others, whether it is called Customer service or human service. One of my favorite quotes is by author Marian Wright Edelman, who said, "Service is the rent we pay for being. It is the very purpose of life, and not something you do in your spare time." However, it is critical that each of us understand the purpose of why we were given this amazing gift of life and what we were put here for, what we are to accomplish in the short time we have. You can't just deliver world-class service at work; it has to be something that is in you, in all areas of your life. It is who you are; it is the way you treat your family, neighbors, coworkers, Customers, and strangers. And remember, there are no strangers, just friends you haven't met yet.

I really like how actor Matthew McConaughey said it, while he accepted the Academy Award for best actor in a leading role for his part in Dallas Buyers Club: "My hero, that's who I chase . . . My hero is me in ten years . . . Every day, every week, every month, every year of my life, my hero is always ten years away. I am never going to be my hero, I am not going to attain that, I know I am not.

That's just fine with me, because that keeps me with somebody to keep on chasing."[71]

Personal purpose statement

Over the last ten years, I have had a personal purpose statement, a vision of what I want to accomplish in my lifetime, and which has served me greatly through good times and some very tough times. I have had this vision posted on my bathroom mirror, it is in my wallet, and it's on my desk in my office. It reads, "Live an extraordinary life so countless others do as well."

I don't want to live an extraordinary life so I have a bigger bank account, nicer car, house, and more toys. I know that if I live an extraordinary life, so many others will as a result. And if I do not find a way to live an extraordinary life, I will probably end up cheating thousands of people.

> Undeveloped potential cheats those around us, those we touch, influence, and impact, as well as deprives ourselves of joy, satisfaction, and opportunities. Living our life to its fullest potential is not an opportunity; it is our responsibility. It is an obligation to be the best version of ourselves we possibly can be, every day. Not just for us and how our life will benefit, but also for all the people depending on us: our spouse, children, friends, employees, coworkers, Customers, and our community.[72]

Living an extraordinary life is living *fully*. I believe that we all have enormous potential inside each of us, and if there are parts of that potential that we do not develop, we are cheating the rest of the world out of the contribution that we could have made.

So if I don't live fully, I don't just deny myself a lot of joy and satisfaction; I deny the rest of the people in the world the benefit of what I could have contributed. Success is when you are firing on all eight cylinders, mentally, physically, emotionally, with family, socially, in your career, financially, and spiritually—all of those are part of you and they all deserve your very best. Living an extraordinary life is like when the flight attendant says, "You must put your own oxygen mask on first before helping those around you." When you first hear that, it actually sounds a bit selfish. However, what use will you be to anyone else if you do not take care of yourself first?

A personal purpose statement is not something you just write out, post, and expect automatic achievement from. You need to make yourself accountable—it needs to be measurable. For me, living an extraordinary life means there are so many things I need to be working on daily, personally, and professionally. It is everything from whom I am spending my time with (are they positive or negative influences in my life?) to my health, exercise, and diet. Some people think that if they eat junk food all day, that is their business. However, I realize that if I eat a poor diet, it is one of the most selfish things I can do. Because when I get home after work, I am going to be exhausted and irritable and not have any good energy left to spend with my boys. Therefore, I just cheated them. It is not only living longer, but it is the quality of life I want to have during my fifties, sixties, and beyond.

Any time I am feeling like I am not living an extraordinary life, and that is more times than I like to admit, I can look at my key drivers and see why—see what I am neglecting—and hopefully I can get right back on track.

Personal		
Personal	Family	Health
Relationships	Self Esteem	Diet
Spiritual	Role Model	Exercise
Give More	Fun	Mind

Professional		
Professional Development	Business	Team
Learning	Vision	Sell Vision
Network	Plan	Opportunity
Goals	Charity	Encouragement

What if today is the last day of your life?

Are you ready? Did you do what you were put on this earth to do? Did you make the impact in people's lives you were capable of? We don't get much say over how or when we die, but we do get to decide how we are going to live, so decide. Is this the life you want to live? Is this the person you want to love? Is this what you want to do every day? Are these the people you want to spend your time with? Is this the best you can be? Can you be stronger, kinder, more compassionate? Can you love more? Can you care more? Can you show more appreciation? Can you forgive? What are you waiting for?

How different would our world be today if Mother Teresa, Gandhi, Martin Luther King, Bill Gates, Walt Disney, Oprah Winfrey, Thomas Edison, Nelson Mandela, and other greats just chose to be ordinary?

Our greatest fear should be that we will not realize our fullest potential before we die.

Did I utilize my potential today?

My greatest fear is that before I die, I won't realize my fullest potential of the talents given to me to use. What a waste if I don't. Think about it: What if God could have given my talents to someone else who would have done more with it? They say a runner has two fears before he runs a race: the first one is that he will not have enough energy to finish the race strong, and the second fear is that he will have some energy left when he finishes. I don't want to have anything left when I am done.

Think for a moment: if you die tomorrow, would you have reached your fullest potential as a spouse, parent, son/daughter, employee, coworker, service provider, leader, neighbor, and friend? The following is an exercise I did that I challenge you to do: ask yourself if you are reaching your fullest potential in all areas of your life. Write a few sentences about each of the people or groups of people that are important to you. Start with "Did I utilize the potential I had inside of me to my . . ."

- spouse?

- children?

- leadership team?

- employees?

- Customers?

- friends?

Below is what I wrote about each group after doing this exercise. I am not this person yet—it is who I want to be. However, when I do read this (try to a few times a week), I do seem to be closer to that person than the days I do not. I hope my examples help you in crafting your own responses.

- Did I utilize the potential I had inside me to make my spouse feel so loved, so beautiful, so sexy and smart every day? Did I remind her what a wonderful mother she is and how fortunate I am to have her as a partner? Did I tell her that I could not be the person I am today if it weren't for the support and love that she continues to give me?

- Did I utilize the potential I had inside me to make my children feel that they were the most special human beings ever born? Did they feel that they could accomplish anything because they believe in their own ability and have phenomenal self-esteem because of the way I make them feel every day?

- Did I utilize the potential I had inside me to inspire leaders to take risks, make them realize that it's all right to fail, to dream? Did I tell them what I think they can accomplish? Did I let them know the greatness I see in them and that there is nothing they can't do?

- Did I utilize the potential I had inside me to help my company achieve its potential? Did I make clear my vision and purpose of why our company exists? Did I find a way to articulate that message to my team and get them to understand the critically important roles they play in that vision? Am I doing everything in my power to make sure the company is on the right path to benefit everyone on the team long term, which will produce plenty of job opportunities, advancement, and both personal and professional fulfillment through their careers?

- Did I utilize the potential I had inside me to help my Customers gain an unfair competitive advantage? Did I deliver more than what they were expecting? Did they feel like I was one of the best investments that they have ever made?

- Did I utilize the potential I had inside me to be a great friend to the people I know well and have known for a long time? Did I make the effort to stay in touch and remind them that I was always there for them, even if we didn't talk but once a year? Did they know that I would drop anything for them in a moment's notice? Did they realize that there was nothing I wouldn't do for them? Did they know that I still enjoyed seeing them, and did I always ask about their families and their work?

I invite you to live an extraordinary life so countless others will. Change the world by creating a customer service revolution.

CUSTOMER SERVICE REVOLUTION

A radical overthrow of conventional business mentality designed to transform what employees and Customers experience. This shift produces a culture that permeates into people's personal lives, at home and in the community, which in turn provides the business with higher sales, morale, and brand loyalty—and which makes price irrelevant.

NOTES

Chapter 1

1 American Customer Satisfaction Index, "Customer Satisfaction with Banks Returns to Pre-recession Level; Health Insurance Improves as Affordable Care Act Kicks In," ACSI LLC, December 10, 2013, http://www.theacsi.org/news-and-resources/press-releases/acsi-press -releases-2013/press-release-december-2013-and-national-Customer -satisfaction-index-q3-2013.

2 "The Dijulius Group's Innovations," www.thedijuliusgroup.com/ innovations/.

3 RightNow Technologies, "2010 Customer Experience Impact Report," Oracle RightNow, Slideshare.net, October 9, 2010, http://www.slideshare .net/RightNow/2010-Customer-experience-impact.

Chapter 2

4 FleishmanHillard, "2012 Digital Influence Index Shows Internet as Leading Influence in Consumer Purchasing Choices," press release for the Digital Influence Index, January 31, 2012, http://fleishmanhillard. com/2012/01/31/2012-digital-influence-index-shows-internet-as-leading -influence-in-consumer-purchasing-choices/.

5 Chris Taylor, "How Social Media are Amplifying Customer Outrage," CNNTech, July 22, 2013, http://www.cnn.com/2011/TECH/social .media/07/22/social.media.outrage.taylor/index.html?_s=PM:TECH.

6 American Customer Satisfaction Index, "Customer Satisfaction with Banks Returns to Pre-recession Level; Health Insurance Improves as Affordable Care Act Kicks In," ACSI LLC, December 10, 2013, http://www.theacsi.org/news-and-resources/press-releases/acsi-press -releases-2013/press-release-december-2013-and-national-Customer -satisfaction-index-q3-2013.

7   CFI Group, "Research Links Customer Satisfaction to Stock Returns," Business Wire press release, July 5, 2012, http://www.businesswire.com /news/home/20120705005269/en/CFI-Group-Research-Links-Customer -Satisfaction-Stock#.UtQUMfbRvzI.

8   Alexander E.M. Hess, "9 Retailers with the Worst Customer Service," USAToday.com, March 16, 2013, http://www.usatoday.com/story/money /business/2013/03/16/9-retailers-worst-Customer-service/1991519/.

9   Shep Hyken, *The Amazement Revolution: Seven Customer Service Strategies to Create an Amazing Customer (and Employee) Experience* (Austin, TX: Greenleaf Book Group, 2011).

10   Rawn Shah, "How Social Business Leaders Lead: Telling the Customer Story Through the Chief Customer Officer," Forbes.com, June 11, 2012, http://www.forbes.com/sites/rawnshah/2012/06/11/how-social-business -leaders-lead-telling-the-customer-story-and-the-chief-customer-officer/.

Chapter 3

11   John R. DiJulius III, *What's the Secret?: To Providing a World Class Customer Experience* (Wiley, 2008).

12   Joshua Rhett Miller, "Spirit Airlines' Boss Calls Industry-high Complaint Rate 'Irrelevant,' Says Dying Veteran Should've Bought Insurance," FOXNews.com, May 3, 2012, http://www.foxnews.com/us/2012/05/03 /spirit-airlines-outpaces-competitors-regarding-passenger-complaints -statistics/.

13   NBC News, "Truth Comes Out: CEO Says Stupid Consumers Deserve Hefty Fees," www.nbcnews.com/tech.

14   Seth Godin, "The Truth about the War for Talent," Seth's Blog, September 18, 2013, http://sethgodin.typepad.com/seths_blog/2013/09/the-truth -about-the-war-for-talent.html.

15   Frank Eliason, *At Your Service: How to Attract New Customers, Increase Sales, and Grow Your Business Using Simple Customer Service Techniques* (Wiley, 2012).

Chapter 4

16   NBC News/Today.com, "Paying Customers Only," NBC News, February 28, 2013, http://www.youtube.com/watch?v=Jo -5uEeIHTA&feature=youtu.be.

17   Image, contributor unknown ,Imgur, http://i.imgur.com/jh38qXT.jpg

18   Anna Almendrala, "Red Medicine Restaurant Shames No-Shows on Twitter," The Huffington Post, March 6, 2013, updated March 27, 2013, http://www.huffingtonpost.com/2013/03/26/red-medicine-no -shows_n_2957271.html.

19 Inquisitr, "Tim Hortons Asthma Attack Scare as Employees Refuse to Let Boy Call 911," Inquisitr.com, March 5, 2013, http://www.inquisitr .com/557538/tim-hortons-asthma-attack-scare-as-employees-refuse-to -let-boy-call-911/.

20 Elise Sole, "Lululemon Test for See-through Yoga Pants Sparks New Outrage," Yahoo! Shine, March 26, 2013, http://shine.yahoo.com/fashion/ -lulu-lemon-says--women-do-not-have-to-bend-over-203021965.html.

21 Lulumon, "Lululemon Blames the Customer for Sheer Yoga Pants," lulumon: a lululemon blogger, July 11, 2013, http://lulumum.blogspot .com/2013/07/lululemon-blames-customer-for-sheer.html.

22 "Every Life Has a Story," www.cathyfamily.com/resources/videos/every -life-has-a-story.aspx.

Chapter 6

23 DiJulius, *What's the Secret?*

24 Ibid.

25 Ibid.

26 Julie Jargon, "Coffee Talk: Starbucks Chief on Prices, McDonald's Rivalry," The Wall Street Journal, Updated March 7, 2011, http://online.wsj.com /news/articles/SB10001424052748704076804576180313111969984?mg=r eno64-wsj&url=http%3A%2F%2Fonline.wsj.com%2Farticle% 2FSB10001424052748704076804576180313111969984.html.

27 Ibid.

28 In Tom Peters, "TP's 'Top 41' Quotes," tompeters.com, 2005, http://www.tompeters.com/blogs/main/PDFs/Quotes41_010306_3.pdf.

29 Dan Pink, "Drive: The Surprising Truth about What Motivates Us," presentation on *RSAnimate*, April 1, 2010.

30 Richard L. Brandt, *Jeff Bezos and the Rise of Amazon.com*, Reprint edition (Portfolio Trade, October 2011).

Chapter 7

31 Joe Schumacker, "No Problem, Big Problem," SpareZ/joeschumacker .com, not dated, http://www.joeschumacker.com/?page_id=48.

Chapter 8

32 Tony Hsieh, *Delivering Happiness: A Path to Profits, Passion, and Purpose*, Edition 1 (New York: Business Plus/Grand Central Publishers, June 2010).

33 DiJulius, *What's the Secret?*

34 Ibid.

35 Transport for London, "Test Your Awareness: Do the Test," YouTube,

March 10, 2008, http://www.youtube.com/watch?v=Ahg6qcgoay4.

36 Walt Disney World, "Unlock the magic with Your Magic Band or Card,"
    https://disneyworld.disney.go.com/plan/my-disney-experience/bands
    -cards/.

37 Claire Cain Miller, "Starbucks and Square to Team Up," The New York
    Times, August 8, 2012, http://www.nytimes.com/2012/08/08/technology
    /starbucks-and-square-to-team-up.html?_r=1&.

38 Stephen Bruce, "Dan Pink: To Sell, Make It Personal," HR Daily Advisor,
    July 29, 2013, http://hrdailyadvisor.blr.com/2013/07/29/dan-pink-to-sell
    -make-it-personal/#.

Chapter 9

39 Kayla Transche, "Wanna See a Teller? Banks Say Pay for It," Financials-
    CNBC.com, August 30, 2013, http://www.cnbc.com/id/100999860.

40 Chip Conley, *Emotional Equations: Simple Steps for Creating Happiness
    + Success in Business + Life* (Atria Books, 2013).

41 John Trent and Gary Smalley, *The Blessing: Giving the Gift of
    Unconditional Love and Acceptance*, revised and updated edition
    (Nashville, TN: Thomas Nelson, 2011).

42 Malcolm Gladwell, *Blink: The Power of Thinking Without Thinking*
    (Back Bay Books, 2007).

43 Gary Vaynerchuk, *The Thank You Economy* (Harper Business, 2011).

44 Nicola Millard, "The Future of Contact Center s in the Age of the
    Customer," B2C, April 10, 2014, http://www.business2community
    .com/customer-experience/future-contact-centers-age-customer
    -0842220#!LeUWJ).

45 Ibid.

Chapter 10

46 Micah Solomon, "What's New About Serving Customers (and What's
    Not)," *HBR Blog Network/Harvard Business Review*, December 10,
    2012, http://blogs.hbr.org/2012/12/whats-new-and-whats-not-about/.

47 Mark Graham Brown, "The Customer Aggravation Index: Predicting
    Customer Loyalty Without Surveys," BusinessFinance, August 24, 2011,
    http://businessfinancemag.com/technology/Customer-aggravation-index
    -predicting-Customer-loyalty-without-surveys.

48 Matthew Dixon, Karen Freeman, and Nicholas Toman, "Stop Trying to
    Delight Your Customers," *Harvard Business Review*, July 2010,
    http://hbr.org/2010/07/stop-trying-to-delight-your-customers.

49 Ibid.

50 Seth Godin, "On Behalf of Yes," Seth's Blog, January 23, 2013, http://sethgodin.typepad.com/seths_blog/2013/01/on-behalf-of-yes.html.

Chapter 11

51 Carmine Gallo, *The Innovation Secrets of Steve Jobs: Insanely Different Principles for Breakthrough Success* (New York: McGraw-Hill, 2010).

52 Hsieh, *Delivering Happiness.*

53 Ibid.

54 Ashley Verrill, "A Zappos Lesson in Customer Service Metrics," *Customer Service Investigator,* June 7, 2012, http://csi.softwareadvice .com/a-zappos-lesson-in-Customer-service-metrics-1101029/.

55 Ibid.

56 Ibid.

57 K. Shelby Skrhak, "Amazon, Kindle, Zappos. What's Next, Jeff Bezos?" *Success,* August 2011.

58 Richard L. Brandt, *One Click: Jeff Bezos and the Rise of Amazon.com* (New York: Portfolio/Penguin, 2011).

59 Geoff Colvin, "How Can American Express Help You?" *CNN Money,* April 19, 2012, http://management.fortune.cnn.com/2012/04/19/ american-express-Customer-service/

60 Hyken, *The Amazement Revolution.*

61 Howard Schultz and Joanne Gordon, *Onward: How Starbucks Fought for Its Life without Losing Its Soul* (Emmaus, PA: Rodale Books, 2011).

62 Stephanie Clifford, "Would You Like a Smile with That?" *The New York Times,* August 6, 2011, http://www.nytimes.com/2011/08/07/business /pret-a-manger-with-new-fast-food-ideas-gains-a-foothold-in-united-states .html?pagewanted=all.

63 Ibid.

64 Ibid.

65 Debbie Millman, "How Starbucks Transformed Coffee from a Commodity into a $4 Splurge," *Fast Company,* September 27, 2011, http://www.fastcompany.com/1777409/how-starbucks-transformed -coffee-commodity-4-splurge.

66 Frances Frei and Anne Morriss, *Uncommon Service: How to Win by Putting Customers at the Core of Your Business* (Boston: Harvard Business Review Press, 2012).

67 Ibid.

68 DiJulius, *What's the Secret?*

69 Van Eden, "Store No. 27 and the Making of QuikTrip," This Land Press, December 6, 2010, http://thislandpress.com/12/06/2010/store-no-27-and -the-making-of-quiktrip/?read=complete.

70 Ibid.

Chapter 12

71 "Explaining Matthew McConaughey's Confounding Acceptance Speech," *Entertainment-Time.com*, March 3, 2014.

72 "My 30 Year Reunion," TheDijuliusGroup.com, a blog by John Dijulius.

ABOUT THE AUTHOR

 As *the* authority on world-class Customer experience, organizations across the world use John's philosophies and methodology for creating world-class service. He has worked with companies such as The Ritz-Carlton, Lexus, Starbucks, Nordstrom, Panera Bread, Nestlé, Marriott Hotel, PWC, Cheesecake Factory, Progressive Insurance, Harley-Davidson, State Farm, Chick-fil-A, and many more to help them continue to raise the bar and set the standard in service that consistently exceeds Customer expectations.

John is the President of The DiJulius Group, a Customer service consulting firm that's purpose is to change the world by creating a Customer service revolution. He is also the founder and owner of John Robert's Spa, an upscale chain (with over 150 employees), which has been named one of the Top 20 Salons in America. John resides in Aurora, Ohio, with his three boys, Johnni, Cal, and Bo.